AF480634

ਰਵਿਦਾਸ
ਠਾਕੁਰ ਬਨਿ ਆਈ

Ravidass Thakur Ban Ai

God Himself Appeared as Ravidass

Toura Vision

Toura Vision — Preserving Wisdom

Toura Vision — Preserving Wisdom

Copyright © 2026 Toura Vision Publishing
All rights reserved.

No part of this publication may be reproduced, stored in a retrieval system, or transmitted in any form or by any means—electronic, mechanical, photocopying, recording, or otherwise—without prior written permission of the publisher, except for brief quotations used in reviews, scholarly works, or academic citation.

This work presents historical research and spiritual reflection. While every effort has been made to ensure accuracy in the presentation of sources and texts, any interpretations or conclusions expressed herein remain those of this work and are offered in a spirit of inquiry and reverence.

Scriptural passages appearing in this volume are presented for educational, historical, and devotional study.

ISBN: 979-8-9956941-1-3

Published by
Toura Vision Publishing

Printed in the United States of America

First Edition — 2026

This journey begins
where academic certainty ends.

From the Publisher

This work is offered as a humble effort to present and reflect upon the Divine Voice preserved in the Ādi Granth.

In keeping with the spirit of the Bāṇī—where Truth is revealed through realization rather than individual authorship—no single author is named. The reflections, interpretations, and arrangement presented here arise from study, contemplation, and reverence for the sacred tradition.

As expressed in the Bāṇī: *Jaisā tū taisā tuhī, kiā upmā dījai* — As You are, so You alone are; what comparison can be given?

What is sought is not newly created, but revealed through the grace of the Satguru. This work, therefore, does not claim ownership over the teachings it explores; it seeks only to serve as a bridge—bringing together scriptural insight, historical understanding, and devotional reflection in a unified voice.

Any limitations in interpretation remain solely our own.

May this offering support the seeker in recognizing the One Light present in all.

Toura Vision Publishing

Contents

Chapter One : Ravi Pargass..1

A New Approach to the Bhaktmal   5

Chapter Two : Religious Transition...7
Chapter Three : Medieval Banaras..9
Chapter Four : The Bhaktmal Tradition..11
Chapter Five : Ramanand: Tradition and Historical Memory.............15
Chapter Six : Ravidass Birth, Chronology, and Historical Context......17
Chapter Seven : Ramanand in the Bhaktmal Memory.......................19
Chapter Eight : Ravidass in the Bhaktmal Memory...........................21
Chapter Nine : Ravidass in the Bhaktmal Commentary of Anantadas 23
Chapter Ten : Ramanand in the Bhaktmal Commentary of Priyadas..27
Chapter Eleven : Ravidass in the Bhaktmal Commentary of Priyadas 29
Chapter Twelve : Beyond Sectarian Lineage.....................................35

Glory of Ravidass & Bhaktamal   41

Chapter Thirteen : The Path of Divine Realism..................................43
Chapter Fourteen : Jhali...45
Chapter Fifteen : Pipa..49
Chapter Sixteen : Dhanna...55
Chapter Seventeen : Mira..61
Chapter Eighteen : Sain..69
Chapter Nineteen : Sadhna...75
Chapter Twenty : Sheikh Farid..77
Chapter Twenty-one : Maharishi Valmiki..79
Chapter Twenty-two : Krishna..81
Chapter Twenty-three : Ravidass...85
Chapter Twenty-four : Kabir..89

Chapter Twenty-five : Jaidev..97
Chapter Twenty-six : Trilochan..99
Chapter Twenty-seven : Namdev..101
Chapter Twenty-eight : Bhaktmal Conclusion...............................107
Chapter Twenty-nine : One Lord Many Names............................111

Adi Granth Akhand Bani   117

Chapter Thirty : Dhur Ki Bani—The Word from the Primal Source 121
Chapter Thirty-one : Satgur Mai Balihari — Ramanand...................129
Chapter Thirty-two : Satgur Hoe Lakhavai — Pipa.........................137
Chapter Thirty-three : Nikat Hau Tum — Mira..............................141
Chapter Thirty-four : Tera Arata — Dhanna..................................149
Chapter Thirty-five : Ghar Ghar Sunia — Sain..............................157
Chapter Thirty-six : Mai Nahi — Sadhna......................................165
Chapter Thirty-seven : Santan Sang — Kabir.................................169
Chapter Thirty-eight : Tu Mero Thakur — Namdev.......................185
 : The Merchant of the Divine Name...201
 : Ardas — The Prayer of the One...202

Origins and Evolution of Gurmukhi Script   203

 : ੧. Punjabi Literary Traditions...205
 : ੨. The Early Spread of Gurmukhi..211
 : ੩. Gurmukhi — The Written Voice of the Divine Bani..................215
 : ੪. Gurmukhi Letters in Ravidass Bani...221
 : Sources Consulted..231

Chapter One

Ravi Pargass

The Radiant Appearance

In the remembered rhythm of sacred time, tradition holds that the Primal Light — the One without beginning or end, the Infinite Consciousness pervading all creation — revealed itself once more within human history. In the year 1377 CE, in the ancient city of Kashi (Banaras, now Varanasi), there was born a child who would come to be known as Ravidass, and through whom the voice of divine compassion would speak with renewed clarity.

Devotional memory associates his birth with Magh Purnima, the full-moon day regarded as auspicious across North India. Later accounts describe the dawn of that day as marked by unusual radiance — a luminous stillness said to have filled the humble dwelling of Santokh Dass and Mata Kalsa Devi. Such narratives are not merely biographical details; they express how the community understood his arrival: not as an ordinary birth alone, but as sacred light entering the simplicity of lived human existence.

The Light, as remembered in tradition, did not descend with royal display or worldly authority. It entered quietly, choosing humility as its dwelling. Born into a family of leather artisans, the child would one day speak words that challenged the boundaries of caste, ritual privilege, and inherited hierarchy. His life would affirm that the Divine is not confined to temple or lineage, but is realized in the truthful and compassionate heart.

Descriptions preserved in later devotional literature speak of a gentle radiance in the infant — a serenity in his gaze and a depth beyond his years. Whether understood as poetic devotion or historical memory, such images reflect the profound impression he would leave upon those who encountered him. Over time, seekers in Kashi and beyond came to recognize in Ravidass a presence that transcended social identity — a voice rooted in the Eternal yet speaking in the living language of the people.

The child was given the name Ravi, signifying the sun — the radiant source of light and life. While some associate the name with Ravivār (Sunday), its deeper spiritual resonance lies in its symbolism. The sun has long served in Indian thought as an image of the self-luminous Reality: impartial, life-giving, sustaining all without distinction. The sacred name Ravi also appears in the Vishnu Sahasranama, the litany of a thousand divine epithets, where it signifies illumination and creative vitality. Whether through scriptural echo or devotional remembrance, the name came to reflect how later generations perceived him — as one whose presence dispelled confusion and awakened clarity.

As he grew, he became known as Ravidass — "servant of the Lord." In this name rests a profound paradox central to the Bhagti vision: the highest realization expresses itself not through domination, but through surrender. The suffix dāss (servant) was embraced by many saints as a mark of humility, affirming that true sovereignty belongs to the Eternal alone. In this sense, the sun remains a fitting metaphor — it gives warmth and life freely, yet claims no reward.

In the sacred geography of Varanasi, the young Ravidass is remembered walking the narrow lanes and river ghats with uncommon composure. Temple bells and ritual rhythms shaped the atmosphere of his early years, yet tradition recalls that even as a child he possessed an inward depth that drew quiet wonder. Those who encountered him sensed not defiance, but a clarity beyond convention.

Later narratives describe him marked outwardly by signs of devotion — the tilak upon the forehead, the fragrance of sandalwood — yet his presence seemed to point beyond external observance. Where many saw stone and ceremony, he spoke of the One Reality dwelling within all beings.

In that era, the sacred thread (janeu) symbolized formal religious discipline and entry into scriptural learning. Over centuries, however, it had also come to signify social separation. In the memory preserved by his followers, Ravidass embodied a deeper teaching: that sanctity lies not in the thread worn upon the body, but in the remembrance carried within the heart. He did not dismiss discipline; he reoriented it. Purity, he taught, arises from truthfulness, compassion, and Naam — the living remembrance of the Divine.

The true thread is the awareness that binds all beings to one source. It does not divide caste from caste, nor restrict sacred speech to a chosen few. In a society where access to learning was often limited, his life and utterance affirmed that every soul carries the right to speak the Divine Name.

As he matured, his spiritual presence extended beyond Kashi. Later traditions recount that even in royal courts such as Chittor, pride softened before the clarity of his insight. Whether among artisans, ascetics, scholars, or rulers, his message remained constant: the same Light shines in every heart.

This vision would later find enduring expression in his bani, preserved in the Adi Granth. There his voice proclaims a truth both simple and profound — that the Divine is neither distant nor exclusive, but nearer than breath and equally present in all. In his celebrated vision of Begampura — the "city without sorrow" — Ravidass described a spiritual commonwealth beyond fear, oppression, and division: a realm defined not by hierarchy but by unity.

Jo ham sehri so meet hamara

"Whoever is a citizen there is my friend."

Where unity is preserved, Begampura appears; where humanity fragments into pride and division, suffering arises.

Thus the life of Ravidass stands at the meeting point of history and sacred remembrance — a life situated in time, yet understood by his followers as the flowering of a Light without origin or end. In him, humility became strength, service revealed sovereignty, and love dissolved the boundaries that separate human from human.

Such was the beginning of a voice that would echo across centuries — calling humanity not to ritual superiority but to unity; not to inherited privilege but to awakened compassion; not to division but to the remembrance of the One Light shining in all.

A New Approach
to the Bhaktmal

Note on Sources, Terminology, and Chronology

Some sources record lifespans in the Vikram Samvat (VS) calendar, which runs approximately 57 years ahead of the Common Era (CE) calendar (about 56 years ahead between January and April), accounting for variations in historical dates.

All personal names in this work are treated with respect; readers may apply honorifics such as Sri, Sant according to their own tradition or preference. For consistency and readability, such titles are not used uniformly throughout the text, and this stylistic choice should not be read as diminishing reverence.

The Bhaktmāl editions and related recensions referenced herein are consulted solely for historical and comparative study, as representative devotional-literary sources. Their inclusion does not imply endorsement of any particular sectarian, doctrinal, or theological position.

All interpretations and reflections presented in this work are offered in a spirit of study and contemplation; any limitations or errors remain solely our own. This work is offered in a spirit of respect for all traditions, seeking understanding rather than dispute.

Chapter Two

Religious Transition

Few texts in Indian religious history reshaped devotional thought as profoundly as the Bhagavata Purana. While traditional belief attributes it to Vyāsa in sacred antiquity, most modern scholars date its composition to between the ninth and tenth centuries CE. Though composed in Sanskrit, its theological vision reflects strong connections to the devotional currents of South India, particularly the Tamil Vaishnava traditions.

The devotional current initiated by the Vaishnava Alvars was later carried forward by a generation of South Indian Acharyas— wandering scholars, poets, and reformers—who, between the eleventh and fifteenth centuries, articulated bhakti as a path both socially inclusive and spiritually transformative. In the late Sultanate period, this vision spread across North India through expanding networks of teachers and disciples, contributing to the formation of an increasingly interconnected devotional landscape.

During the Mughal era—particularly under Akbar—a climate of relative political stability and religious accommodation allowed Vaishnava institutions to flourish under both imperial and Rajput patronage. Temples, pilgrimage centers, and regional congregational communities expanded across North India, especially in the sacred Braj region. The Bhaktmāls, Charitas, and Vārtās composed in the seventeenth and eighteenth centuries reflect this close association between rulers and saints—a period in which religious life, cultural production, and political authority briefly intersected in rare alignment.

Yet this alignment also marked a transition. As sacred expression moved from village gatherings into courts and established institutions, its language became increasingly systematized, its lineages more formally defined, and its saints more carefully categorized. What had begun as a radical interior awakening gradually entered the framework of tradition and memory.

At the same time, the traditional and often exclusive study of Sanskrit śāstras remained largely confined to Brahmin scholars, concentrating scriptural authority within a narrow custodial circle and limiting access across caste and gender lines. It was within this structured and hierarchical environment that a new vernacular voice began to take shape in North India. Ravidass and the circle of Sant figures associated with him did not compose in scholastic Sanskrit, nor did they ground authority in institutional lineage. Instead, they articulated realized truth in the living speech of the people—accessible to artisans, laborers, householders, and women alike. In this widening of sacred expression, figures such as Mirabai would later be recognized not by birth or gender, but by the depth of realized utterance. In the voice of Ravidass, sacred speech assumed written form in a new way—preserved not as elite commentary, but as direct spiritual expression. Here, devotion was no longer mediated through scholastic custodianship; it emerged as lived utterance, accessible to all.

Chapter Three

Medieval Banaras

Banaras—eternal city of light—has long stood at the crossroads of faith and empire. Yet from the 13th to the 15th centuries, its sanctity was tested by waves of conquest that swept across northern India. The armies of Muḥammad Ghori, Iltutmish (r. 1210–1236), Firoz Shah Tughlaq (r. 1351–1388), and later the Sharqi rulers of Jaunpur, notably Mahmud Shah Sharqi (r. 1447), plundered the sacred city, turning temples to rubble and raising mosques in their place. Each time the people rebuilt, destruction followed again—most fiercely under Sikandar Lodi (r. 1489–1517), whose zeal left deep scars on Kashi's spiritual landscape.

Yet the light of Banaras could not be extinguished. With the coming of Emperor Akbar (r. 1556–1605), a new spirit of tolerance began to heal the city's wounds. His finance minister, Raja Todar Mal, guided by the Narayan Bhaṭṭa, oversaw the reconstruction of the Visvanatha Temple (1584–1585), restoring to Kashi its beating heart of devotion. But this revival, too, proved fragile. Shah Jahan (r. 1628–1658) attempted to destroy the temple but failed; later, Aurangzeb, through his Farman of April 18, 1669, ordered its complete demolition—a decree carried out on September 2, 1669.

Even so, faith endured. By the late eighteenth century, Banaras once again stirred with restoration and hope. Between 1752 and

1777, leaders such as Dattoji Scindia and Malhar Rao Holkar led efforts to rebuild the holy site. Their vision reached fulfillment when Queen Ahilyabai Holkar of Indore (r. 1776–1778) undertook the full reconstruction of the Kashi Visvanatha Temple, reviving the sacred pulse of the city.

The nineteenth century brought new trials under British administration (1809–1811), when Hindu devotees faced restrictions on temple control. Yet worship continued, and expansions at the Adi Vishveshvara and Radha–Krishna shrines kept the continuity of Kashi's spiritual life unbroken.

The story reached a golden culmination in the early nineteenth century, when Maharaja Ranjit Singh, the ruler of Punjab, donated tons of gold to plate the domes of the Kashi Vishwanath Temple, earning it the name Suvarna Vishvanatha—the "Golden Temple of Kashi." His act of devotion transcended sectarian lines: the same ruler had earlier gilded the Harmandir Sahib at Amritsar, widely known as the Golden Temple, as well as the Keshav Deo Temple and the Jagannath Temple—binding the sacred geography of India in a shared radiance of faith.

The city itself, known historically as Kashi—"the City of Light"—and later widely called Banaras or Benares, is today officially named Varanasi, though all three names continue to appear across historical and devotional literature.

Chapter Four

The Bhaktmal Tradition

The term Bhaktmal literally means "Garland of Devotees." It was not composed as a historical chronicle in the modern sense, but as a devotional anthology—poetic, symbolic, and often compressed in expression. Its purpose was remembrance and inspiration rather than strict chronology. The work consists of brief verses, each offering a distilled portrait of a saint's spiritual character rather than a detailed biographical account.

By the time the Bhaktmal was composed in the late sixteenth century, the Sant movement of North India—represented by figures such as Ravidass, Kabir, and others—had already transformed devotional life. Their teachings, expressed in vernacular language and centered on direct experience of the Divine, had spread widely across social and regional boundaries. The impulse to gather and preserve their remembrance in a literary garland arose only after their influence had become firmly established within the devotional consciousness of the people.

The principal compilers and commentators of the Bhaktmāl tradition emerged from circles associated with the Ramanandi Sampradaya. The tradition itself took shape in the late sixteenth century with the work of Nabhadas, whose Bhaktmāl (c. 1585 CE) became a foundational Vaishnava text composed in the Braj–Awadhi literary milieu. Arranging the lives of more than two hundred saints and devotees into a systematic devotional compilation, Nabhadas offered not extended biographies but concise poetic sketches that highlighted the inner qualities and spiritual stature of each figure.

In the original recension attributed to Nabhadas, the entry on Ravidass appears among the early group of saints, indicating his recognized prominence within the devotional memory of the period. Nabhadas portrays him as spiritually discerning—one able to "separate milk from water," a classical metaphor for distinguishing truth from falsehood. Such characterization suggests that he was remembered not merely as a devotee, but as a figure of moral clarity and spiritual authority.

Nabhadas's work was soon followed by Anantadas, who composed an early ṭika (c. 1588 CE). In the earliest recensions attributed to Anantadas, saints are presented primarily through devotional qualities rather than rigid sectarian classification; the emphasis remains experiential, where the presence of the saint outweighs formal theological labeling.

In the eighteenth century, Priyadas produced a more elaborate commentary (c. 1712 CE), expanding the brief poetic portraits into fuller narratives enriched with theological reflection. This interpretive tradition was continued by Raghavdas and others, whose writings increasingly reflected the developed Vaishnava theology of their time. Within this broader devotional milieu, Ramanandi thinkers such as Tulsidas contributed to shaping the intellectual and spiritual atmosphere in which the Bhaktmāl tradition was preserved and interpreted.

As the Bhaktmāl passed from generation to generation, devotional memory gradually intertwined with theological interpretation. What began as poetic remembrance evolved into layered

12

commentary reflecting the intellectual, sectarian, and social worlds of successive eras. To read the Bhaktmāl attentively, therefore, is to encounter not a single fixed voice, but a living tradition shaped across centuries by reverence, interpretation, and devotion.

Chapter Five

Ramanand: Tradition and Historical Memory

According to traditional accounts, Ramanand was born in 1299 CE at Prayag (modern Allahabad) on the seventh day of Kṛṣṇa Pakṣa in the month of Māgha, and is said to have passed away in 1410 CE on the third day of Vaiśākha Śukla. These dates are preserved in the chronicles of the Ramavat Sampradaya and related Vaishnava traditions. Early devotional sources, including references attributed to the Agastya Saṁhitā, identify his parents as Punyasadan and Sushila.

In his formative years, Ramanand is described as having studied the Vedas, Puranas, and Śāstras at Prayag, receiving training within the orthodox discipline associated with the Sri Sampradaya of South India, particularly the centers of Srirangam and Kanchipuram. Formed within this theological and ritual framework, he adhered to its codes of scholarship, renunciation, and devotional practice. Tradition further records that he later settled in Banaras, where his influence expanded within North India.

Recorded Dates and Scholarly Mentions

Several early scholars and historians have acknowledged the traditional lifespan of Ramanand as 1299–1410 CE. The Indologist R. G. Bhandarkar referred to Vaishnava sources that record Ramanand's birth in Vikram Samvat 1356 (1299 CE) and his passing in 1467 (1410 CE). Similarly, linguist George Abraham Grierson observed that popular tradition places Ramanand's death in 1410 A.D., noting the unusually long lifespan attributed to him.

The Hindi literary historian K. C. Barthwal, in The Nirguna School of Hindi Poetry, also accepted these traditional dates based on earlier devotional sources. Contemporary devotional institutions, including organizations such as BAPS Swaminarayan Sanstha, continue to preserve the same chronological framework in their presentations.

While modern academic scholarship has debated aspects of Ramanand's chronology, the consistency of these traditional references demonstrates the strength and continuity of his remembered lifespan within Vaishnava devotional memory.

Chapter Six

Ravidass Birth, Chronology, and Historical Context

The memory of Ravidass has long been preserved in devotional verse as well as historical tradition. Among the couplets commonly associated with him are:

Jat-pat puchhe nahi koi,
Har ko bhajai so Har ka hoi.

Chaudah sau taintīs ki, Māgh sudī pandrās,
Dukhiyōṁ ke kalyāṇ hit, pragate Sri Ravidāss.

The first affirms the spiritual principle that caste and birth hold no value before devotion; the second records the traditional year of his appearance.

According to longstanding devotional tradition, Ravidass was born in Vikram Samvat 1433 (1377 CE) on the full-moon day of the month of Māgh (Magh Purnima). Some traditions further note that this date fell on a Sunday. This reckoning has been preserved within community memory and later hagiographical sources.

When converted into the Common Era calendar, Vikram Samvat 1433 corresponds to 1377 CE. Modern scholarship generally places Ravidass within the late fourteenth and fifteenth centuries, in broad harmony with this traditional reckoning. Scholars such as Hazari Prasad Dwivedi, R. G. Bhandarkar, K. C. Barthwal, Charlotte Vaudeville, and David N. Lorenzen have likewise situated him within this general chronological framework, though precise dates remain a matter of scholarly discussion.

This dating aligns with the historical milieu of North India during the late Delhi Sultanate period and allows for the devotional associations traditionally drawn between Ravidass, Ramanand, and later figures such as Mirabai.

Chapter Seven

Ramanand in the Bhaktmal Memory

The portrayal of Ramanand in the Bhaktmal of Nabhadas reflects the devotional imagination of the late sixteenth century. In poetic form, composed in the Braj vernacular, Nabhadas writes:

जब लहि यवन अनीति धरा व्याकुल भइ भारी ।
यति कृपालु रघुनाथ तबहिं मुनि रूप सँवारी ॥
जैन बौद्ध मत नाशि याविनी अनय विनासे ।
भगवद्धर्म प्रचारि सु वैष्णव तत्व प्रकाशे ॥
शिष्य द्वादशीदित्य सम ज्ञान किरण जग तम हरे ।
रामानन्दाचार्य कर धर्मध्वजा धर धर जग फरहरे ॥

Jab lahi Yavan aneeti dharā, vyākul bhayi bhārī,
Yati kripālu Raghunāth tabahiṁ, muni rūp sanvārī.
Jain Bauddh mat nāshi, Yāvinī anay vināse,
Bhagavad dharm prachāri su, Vaishnav tattva prakāse.
Shishya dvādash āditya sam, jñān kiraṇ jag tam hare,
Rāmānand Āchārya kar, dharm dhwajā dhar dhar jag pharhare.

In these verses, Ramanand is depicted as a divinely inspired teacher who appeared during a time of moral and religious upheaval. The imagery suggests that when disorder spread across the land, the compassionate Lord assumed the form of a sage to restore dharma. Rival traditions—such as Jain, Buddhist, and what the text calls Yavana influences—are poetically described as being overcome, while the essence of Vaishnava devotion is said to have been reestablished.

The metaphor of his twelve disciples shining like twelve suns emphasizes not literal cosmology, but the expansion of spiritual knowledge through discipleship. The raising of the "banner of dharma" symbolizes the consolidation of a devotional lineage rather than political conquest.

Such language reflects the sectarian and theological environment of the sixteenth century, in which devotional communities often articulated their identity through poetic triumph over competing traditions. Read in this light, the passage reveals how Ramanand was remembered—as a reformer who revitalized devotion and whose disciples radiated spiritual illumination across North India.

Chapter Eight

Ravidass in the Bhaktmal Memory

In the Bhaktmal of Nabhadas, Ravidass is portrayed as a
spiritually authoritative and reformative figure. In poetic form,
composed in the Braj vernacular, the poet writes:

वर्णाश्रम अभिमान यानि द्विज बाद किये बहु ।
दे श्रुति शास्त्र प्रमाण कह्यो हरि भक्ति सबहि गहु ॥
पारस द हरि लीन्ह परीक्षा तबहुँ डिगे नहिं ।
काम क्रोध कलि जित्यो संत गुरु राम कृपा लहि ॥
भक्तहिं जाति न शिष्य बनि, मीरा, झाली मंत्र लिय ।
रविदास बनि धर्म पति, भक्ति महात्म्य दिखाइ दिय ॥

Varṇāśram abhimān yāni, dvij bād kiye bahu,
De śruti śāstra pramāṇ kahyo, Hari bhakti sabahi gahu.
Pāras da Hari līnh parīkṣhā, tabahuṁ ḍige nahiṁ,
Kām krodh kali jityo, sant guru Rām kṛpā lahi.
Bhaktahīn jāti na śiṣya bani, Mīrā, Jhālī mantra liy,
Ravidāss bani dharma pati, bhakti mahātmya dikhāi diy.

In this passage, Ravidass is presented as opposing the pride
associated with varṇāśrama hierarchy and the disputes of the
learned "twice-born." Appealing to the authority of Śruti and

Śāstra, he is said to have urged all people alike to embrace devotion to Hari.

The reference to the "Pāras" (philosopher's stone) reflects a common devotional motif in which divine testing confirms spiritual steadfastness. The verse further attributes to him mastery over desire and anger—symbolic of conquering the forces of Kaliyuga through divine grace.

Significantly, the text associates him with figures such as Mirabai and the Rajput princess traditionally identified as Jhālī. This reflects the widespread memory of Ravidass as a spiritual guide whose influence crossed both caste and royal boundaries.

The closing line describes him as a "dharma pati," a phrase that may be understood not as political sovereignty but as moral-spiritual authority within the devotional imagination of the period. Through this portrayal, the Bhaktmal situates Ravidass among the foremost figures of the Bhakti tradition, emphasizing equality, steadfastness, and transformative grace.

Chapter Nine

Ravidass in the Bhaktmal Commentary of Anantadas

The early commentary tradition of Anantadas expands the brief poetic references of Nabhadas into fuller narrative form. In his account, Ravidass is described in explicitly incarnational language:

Ravidāss līyo Avatārā —

"Ravidass took birth as an incarnation."

The setting is Banaras (Kashi), portrayed as the most sacred of cities, where divine grace is ever-present and liberation assured. The verse underscores the sanctity of the place as the divinely prepared setting for his appearance.

Story of Birth

Ravidass took divine birth in Banaras, as declared in the Sruti and Smriti. As an infant, he refused milk and cried unceasingly, until divine grace intervened. In a vision, Lord Hari revealed to Ramanand that this child was a devoted soul reborn — once a Brahmin who had heard the scriptures but failed to renounce meat and was now born among leather-workers to complete his spiritual journey. At Hari's command, Ramanand came, blessed the family, and touched the child's head; at once, Ravidass became calm and began to nurse. The city rejoiced, homes were adorned, and Anantadas concludes that even the Lord rejoices in telling of Ravidass's birth in Kashi — the holiest of cities and the crown of all men.

Childhood and Work

In devotional accounts, divine grace is said to have guided Ravidass from an early age. By childhood, he is described as having embraced the nine forms of bhakti and as walking steadfastly in the path of his Satguru. One day, while engaged in his humble work, the Lord appeared to test him and asked how he endured such poverty. Ravidass replied, *"My only treasure is You, before whom even Lakshmi bows."* Pleased, Hari offered him a philosopher's stone said to turn iron into gold, but Ravidass gently refused, knowing that true devotion needs no gold to shine.

Missing Ramanand in the Story

As Ravidass's fame spread through his songs of divine love, accounts describe people gathering in great numbers to hear him. His growing renown is said to have unsettled sections of the Brahmin community in Banaras, who questioned the legitimacy of his worship. Yet in these narratives, the figure of Acharya Ramanand—himself a Brahmin—is notably absent. If Ramanand truly lived in Banaras at the same time, his silence in this episode remains unexplained.

Ravidass and Jhali

According to devotional tradition, in the royal city of Chittor lived Queen Jhali—wise and virtuous, yet without a Satguru. Hearing of Ravidass, whom devotees revered as reflecting the Divine presence of Krishna, the Avatar of Vishnu, dwelling in Kashi, she set out to seek him. After first meeting Kabir, she journeyed to Ravidass's home.

There, she beheld what tradition describes as a radiant temple of devotion—filled with music, fragrance, and the praise of Govind. Among the gathered saints sat Ravidass, shining with divine presence, his words said to be sweeter than nectar. In that moment, all royal pride fell away, and the queen bowed at his feet. With a gentle touch upon her head, the Satguru bestowed the grace her soul had long sought.

Togetherness of Ravidass, Kabir, and Sain

After Queen Jhali offered generous gifts for the service of the devotees and returned to her kingdom, she directed that her wealth be used for celebrations in Hari's name. That night, Kashi is said to have echoed with unrest as a great crowd gathered in confusion. In devotional accounts, Ravidass, Kabir, and Sain are remembered as coming together at that moment to restore peace —their shared presence calming the people and settling troubled hearts.

Ravidass, the Omnipresent Presence

According to devotional tradition, when Queen Jhali invited Ravidass to Chittor, a grand feast was arranged in his honor. The Brahmins, unsettled by his presence, demanded that they be served first. As they sat to eat, each is said to have witnessed a wonder—beside every Brahmin appeared the same serene presence of Ravidass. In that moment, pride gave way to humility, and they fell at his feet, crying,

"You are the Satguru."

Casting aside their sacred threads, they sought his blessing. With compassion, Ravidass raised his hands and blessed them all. The king, the queen, and the people of Chittor rejoiced, for through this vision the light of truth dispelled all distinction—revealing no separation between the Lord and Ravidass.

Chapter Ten

Ramanand in the Bhaktmal Commentary of Priyadas

In the early eighteenth century, Priyadas expanded the Bhaktmal tradition into a more elaborate theological narrative. In his commentary, Ramanand is portrayed in exalted terms:

श्रीरामानन्द रघुनाथ सम, द्वितीय सेतु जग तारक भयो ॥

अनन्तानन्द, कबीर, सुखा, सुरसुरा, पद्मावती, नरहरि,

पीपा, भावानन्द, रैदास, धन्ना, सेन — सुरसुर गृह हरि ॥

और शिष्य-प्रशिष्य अनेक, एक से एक उजागर भयो ॥

जग-मंगल आधार यह, भक्ति दशधा के आगार भयो ॥

बहु काल तनु धारण करि, प्रणत जनन को पार दियो ॥

श्रीरामानन्द रघुनाथ सम, द्वितीय सेतु जग तारक भयो ॥

Shri Rāmānand Raghunāth sam, dvitīya setu jag tārak bhayo,
Anantānand, Kabīr, Sukhā, Surasurā, Padmāvatī, Narahari
Pīpā, Bhāvānand, Raidās, Dhannā, Sen — Surasur gr̥h Hari.
Aur shishya-prashishya anek, ek se ek ujāgar bhayo,
Jag-mangal ādhār yeh, bhakti dashadhā ke āgār bhayo.
Bahu kāl tanu dhāraṇ kari, praṇat janan ko pār diyo,
Shri Rāmānand Raghunāth sam, dvitīya setu jag tārak bhayo.

Priyadas compares Ramanand to Lord Raghunath (Rama), describing him as a "second bridge" (dvitīya setu) for the world — a metaphor evoking the mythic bridge built by Rama to cross the ocean. Through this imagery, Ramanand is presented as a spiritual savior who ferries souls across the ocean of worldly existence.

The verse also enumerates his principal disciples, including figures such as Kabir, Pipa, Ravidass, Dhanna, and Sain. By formally listing these saints within a unified lineage, Priyadas strengthens the institutional identity of the Ramanandi tradition.

The closing lines emphasize the expansion of disciples and sub-disciples, portraying the lineage as a reservoir of devotion and a foundation for the welfare of the world. Such language reflects not merely biography, but the consolidation of a devotional order in the early eighteenth century.

Chapter Eleven

Ravidass in the Bhaktmal Commentary of Priyadas

In the early eighteenth century, Priyadas further expanded the devotional memory of Ravidass, presenting him in language of philosophical and spiritual authority. The verse reads:

सदाचार श्रुति-शास्त्र-वचन सँग, अविरुद्ध वाणी उचारि ।
क्षीर-नीर विवेक धरि, परमहंस सम अगाध विचारि ॥
भगवत-कृपा प्रतापे सो, परम-पद तन हीं पायो ।
राज-सिंहासन आसन धरि, जग में ज्ञान प्रकाश दिखायो ॥
वर्णाश्रम-अभिमान त्यागि, चरण-रज करि नमन कियो ।
संदेह-ग्रंथि-भंजन-पटु, निर्मल वचन रविदास कियो ॥

Sadāchār śruti-shāstra-vachan sang, aviruddh vāṇī uchāri,
Kṣhīr-nīr vivek dhari, paramhans sam agādh vichāri.
Bhagavat-kṛpā pratāpe so, param-pad tan hīṁ pāyo,
Rāj-siṁhāsan āsan dhari, jag meṁ gyān prakāś dikhāyo.
Varṇāśram-abhimān tyāgi, charaṇ-raj kari naman kiyo,
Sandeh-granthi-bhanjan-paṭu, nirmal vachan Raidās kiyo.

Priyadas portrays Ravidass as speaking in harmony with Śruti and Śāstra, emphasizing moral integrity (sadāchār) and doctrinal coherence. The phrase kṣhīr-nīr vivek—the ability to distinguish milk from water—evokes the classical image of the paramhansa, the realized sage capable of discerning truth from illusion.

He is further described as attaining the param pad (supreme state) "within the body itself," a formulation resonant with both Bhakti and Sant traditions that affirm liberation while living. The imagery of a royal throne (rāj-siṁhāsan) symbolizes not political sovereignty but spiritual sovereignty—knowledge radiating outward to illuminate the world.

Significantly, Priyadas emphasizes Ravidass's renunciation of varṇāśrama pride and his humility before the divine. The final line celebrates him as a master capable of cutting the knots of doubt, whose speech is described as pure and stainless.

Birth Narrative in Priyadas: Guru Authority and Karmic Logic

In his later Bhaktmāl commentary, Priyādās offers a markedly different account of Ravidass's birth. He narrates that a celibate disciple of Ramananda once brought a small offering of flour from a place the Guru had forbidden. Viewing the offering as impure, Ramanand pronounced a curse, declaring that the disciple would be born in a lower caste in his next life.

According to this account, the child—born as Ravidass—retained the memory of his past service, refusing milk even from his mother. Upon hearing a divine voice, Ramanand recognized the severity of his own action and came to the child's parents, who pleaded for relief. Only then did the child drink milk and survive, though Priyādās adds that the Guru's heart remained burdened by the memory of the curse.

This narrative reflects a theological framework centered on guru authority and karmic consequence, in which social birth is explained through moral causality. While honoring Ravidass's spiritual stature, the account simultaneously reinterprets his birth within caste-bound logic—revealing more about the concerns of later Vaishnava tradition than about Ravidass's own teaching, which consistently denies birth, occupation, or impurity as measures of divine realization.

Childhood and Work

In Priyādās's telling, the childhood and work of Ravidass are shaped into a devotional ideal, emphasizing renunciation, service, and repeated divine testing rather than social or historical detail. Ravidass grew up with deep love for the servants of Hari (God's devotees). His father gave him no support and turned him away from every place. All the family wealth and property were given to his stepmother; his father, being under her influence, separated him completely. The household servants were bound by loyalty and revealed nothing. Once, when Ramadas came home, he made sandals from raw leather and offered them carefully to a saint. Then he gave up all attachment, built a small, thatched hut, and remained there, devoted to service — sharing whatever he received with the holy saints.

He endured great suffering, yet his heart remained filled with joy and devotion. Beloved Hari (God) Himself came, assuming the form of a devotee. He honored Ramadas greatly, eating and drinking with satisfaction, and then, like a touchstone, He tested him and kept watch over him. Ramadas said, *"My wealth is only Rama; stones and gold are the same to me. I desire neither riches nor comfort — I only wish to offer my body and life in devotion."* When Hari offered him gold, Ramadas said, *"I have no use for it; please keep it safe, keep this hut instead, and take away what is impure."*

After some time, the Lord again came in the same form — thirteen months had passed. With love He spoke, saying, *"Tell me, what is the way of the touchstone (pāras)?" "Take this place,"* He said, *"but my heart is not content. Do whatever you wish, for I now seek only Your protection."* The Lord smiled and suddenly vanished — listen, this is the wondrous play! In service He received five gold coins every day, yet he never wavered in his faith. While serving, he felt fear in his heart at night, and the Lord said to him, *'Give up your stubbornness — keep your devotion pure, for through your surrender lies My victory.'*

Ravidass Standing Alone

In Priyādās's account, Ravidass serves Lord Hari with quiet devotion within his humble home, unconcerned with worldly praise or display. Inspired inwardly by the Divine, his presence nonetheless unsettles the proud Brahmins, who complain against him before the king. Summoned to the royal court, Ravidass is judged rightly, and the king entrusts the matter to God Himself. Through this divine play, Ravidass's glory is said to spread throughout the world, and even those who once opposed him come to accept him as a Satguru.

Notably, in this episode—despite its public setting and the involvement of royal authority—the figure of Ramanand does not appear. Ravidass stands alone, upheld not by lineage or mediation, but by the force of devotion itself, like a jewel that shines even when kept in a closed chest.

Ravidass and Jhali: Without Companions

In Priyādās's narrative, in the city of Chittor there lived a queen named Jhali. Upon hearing the name of Ravidass, a deep longing arose in her heart, and she became his devoted disciple. Some Brahmins, seeing this, grew envious and brought their complaint before the king. Seeking justice, the king took his seat and ordered that the accused be summoned.

As the Brahmins recited verses from the Vedas and sang hymns in pride, the Lord Himself is said to have appeared beside Ravidass, seating him close and accepting his devotion. Notably, in this public and royal setting, Kabir and Sain do not appear in Priyādās's account. Ravidass stands alone, upheld not by the presence of fellow saints, but by divine witness itself.

Ravidass is Omnipresent and Janju

When Queen Jhali returned to her kingdom, she sent word again, saying, *"As I have honored you before, please come and bless us once more."* Ravidass came himself, accompanied by his disciples, bearing only a simple cloth and a spirit of humility. Hearing of his arrival, some Brahmins resolved to bar his way. A meal was prepared, and they sat down to eat; Ravidass too was seated among the gathering, and the king watched him attentively in the midst of all.

In that moment, tradition says, a deeper vision dawned. Ravidass was perceived everywhere at once, as though countless presences appeared together, dissolving all separation. What had been seen as difference was revealed as oneness, and the assembly beheld Ravidass not apart from them, but present within all.

It is in Priyādās's later telling that Ravidass is further described as removing a golden thread from his body, revealing not caste or ornament, but a radiant presence beyond distinction. Earlier accounts do not record this image. In later devotional retellings, Raghavdās presents the episode in a more elaborate poetic form, describing the sacred thread as emerging from the shoulder itself. In certain Punjabi singing traditions associated with Bhaktmal followers, the motif appears in even more expanded imagery, sometimes multiplying the threads as signs of spiritual authority. These variations reflect the evolving devotional imagination of different regions and communities rather than a fixed historical memory.

Yet across these tellings, one truth remains constant: what shines is not thread, caste, or ornament, but the Divine Light equally present in all.

Chapter Twelve

Beyond Sectarian Lineage

Within the Bhaktmāl tradition, Ravidass cannot be understood as a mere bead in a garland of saints. Rather, he emerges as the central bead — the silent axis around which the garland itself is arranged. The earliest Bhaktmāl, composed by Nabhadās in 1585 CE, and the subsequent recension by Anantadās around 1588 CE, place Ravidass within the broad current of the Bhakti movement without fixing him into a single sectarian identity.

As noted by Winand M. Callewaert in The Hagiographies of Anantadās, numerous seventeenth-century manuscripts and printed versions of these texts exist, each differing in detail — especially in their portrayals of Ravidass and his followers. These variations are not minor; they reflect ongoing attempts to reinterpret, reframe, and sometimes absorb Ravidass into later devotional hierarchies.

More than a century later, Priyādās (1712 CE) produced a new commentary that significantly altered earlier depictions. His narratives concerning Ravidass diverge sharply from those of Anantadās, revealing how sectarian retellings reshaped the memory of the early Bhakti era. Where Anantadās had earlier spoken of Ravidass taking divine birth in Banaras, later recensions introduced karmic explanations, including claims of rebirth tied to dietary transgression. Priyādās went further still, presenting an entirely new story in which Ravidass appears as a former disciple who disobeyed Ramanand and was reborn due to a curse.

Such contradictions across sixteenth to eighteenth-century Bhaktmāl literature do not clarify Ravidass's identity — they destabilize it. When a single figure repeatedly resists fixed classification, while narratives around him continue to multiply and shift, it suggests that the tradition is grappling with a presence larger than its categories.

What emerges from this comparison is not a consistent biography, but a consistent reality: Ravidass stands apart from lineage-making, rebirth-justifying, and sect-preserving frameworks. Beneath these evolving legends lies a deeper truth — that Ravidass functioned not merely as a saint within the Bhakti movement, but as a transformative presence whose authority could not be safely contained within inherited religious structures.

The Childhood Accounts of Ravidass: A Comparative View

According to the parcaīs of Anantadās, Ravidass exhibited exceptional spiritual resolve even in early childhood. At the age of seven—when Brahmin boys customarily received the janeū (sacred thread)—he is said to have refused the ritual, asserting that purity does not arise from an external symbol but from devotion to God. This moment marks his earliest recorded challenge to caste-based authority and ritual hierarchy, affirming the primacy of inner realization over inherited status. Beyond this, Anantadās offers little biographical detail, noting only that Ravidass continued in humble labor and service to humanity.

Priyādās, writing more than a century later in 1712 CE, presents a markedly different account. He introduces the figure of a stepmother who allegedly seized the family's wealth, compelling Ravidass into poverty and manual work. This episode, absent from earlier sources, appears to reflect a later interpretive tendency to frame Ravidass's life through moralized suffering. Its late appearance raises questions about how such personal details entered the tradition long after his lifetime.

Despite these divergences, both Anantadās and Priyādās preserve one striking and consistent element: God Himself, appearing in the guise of a devotee, visits Ravidass. This shared motif is significant. Across otherwise conflicting narratives, the presence of the Divine is not mediated through institutions or intermediaries, but approaches Ravidass directly. Such convergence suggests that the tradition struggled to articulate an experience that exceeded conventional categories—that Ravidass was not merely a recipient of divine grace, but the locus through which that grace was revealed. In simplicity and humility, these stories present him as embodying the very principles he taught: love without distinction, equality without hierarchy, and liberation accessible to all.

Truth Beneath the Bhaktmāl

Anantadās narrates the well-known episode of the philosopher's stone. God, appearing in the guise of a humble devotee, visits Ravidass and offers him a parās—a stone believed to transform iron into gold. Ravidass, unmoved by the promise of material wealth, asks that it be wrapped in cloth and placed in the thatch of his hut. When the devotee returns thirteen months later, the stone remains exactly where it was left—untouched, its power rendered meaningless before a soul already content in divine realization.

Priyādās retells this same account with embellishment. In this version, the devotee touches the stone to Ravidass's iron awl, which instantly turns to gold. Yet even here, Ravidass remains indifferent, remarking that he already possesses the true treasure —the wealth of the Divine Name. Once again, the stone is placed in the thatch, and when the devotee returns a year later, it remains unused and forgotten.

These variations reveal more about the intentions of later commentators than about Ravidass himself. The miracle is repeatedly expanded, yet the central message remains unchanged: material transformation holds no value for one who has realized the Divine. Through metaphor and symbol, the Bhaktmāl tradition attempts to express a truth that resists literal description —that divine presence is not demonstrated through spectacle, but through detachment, humility, and inner fullness.

What endures beneath these shifting narratives is a consistent vision of God not as distant or selective, but as present within every being. Ravidass's teaching affirms that the Divine makes no distinction between high and low, rich and poor, man and woman —all stand equal before the One Light. His life repeatedly redirects attention away from supernatural display and toward awakened humanity.

This same understanding appears in the account of Queen Ratan Jhālī, who encountered Ravidass's radiance not as sorcery or wonder, but as an experience of love and transformation. Such stories suggest that Ravidass's purpose was never to exhibit power, but to awaken compassion, nonviolence, and unity—the living essence of Dharma.

Changing Narratives

In later Bhaktmāl recensions, the stories of Ravidass and his contemporaries—Kabir, Sain, Dhannā, and others—appear in increasingly divergent and reshaped forms. Some versions omit Ramanand altogether, while others amplify his influence in ways that reflect emerging sectarian priorities rather than historical continuity. Over time, variations in naming also begin to surface, with Ravidass rendered as Raidas, Ramdas, or Ramadas in certain manuscripts and printed editions. Alongside these changes, saints once remembered as close companions of Ravidass are gradually reduced, altered, or omitted entirely.

Such shifts point less to historical clarification and more to evolving editorial agendas. As devotional traditions were reorganized, figures who did not fit neatly within later frameworks were either absorbed, reattributed, or quietly displaced. The result is a layered hagiographic record in which the same saint appears differently depending on the theological and institutional concerns of the period in which a given version was produced.

In the earliest accounts, the gosṭī—the spiritual assemblies and dialogues—between Kabir and Ravidass explicitly include Sain, reflecting a shared current of devotion rooted in equality and lived realization. Later retellings, however, increasingly separate these figures, fragmenting what was once presented as a united spiritual fellowship. Historically, such divisions hold little ground. Ravidass and Kabir were contemporaries, active within the same devotional horizon, speaking not as rival voices but as expressions of a single Bhakti impulse that challenged hierarchy, ritual exclusivity, and inherited status.

The persistence of these early associations, even as later versions attempt to rearrange them, suggests that the original memory of this shared spiritual community proved difficult to erase. What changes across the Bhaktmāl traditions is not the ethical or devotional core of their teaching, but the narrative structures used to contain it.

Conclusion: The Hidden Light Preserved

Across centuries of Bhaktmāl retellings, the presence of Ravidass was repeatedly reshaped within competing sectarian frameworks. His stature was often softened into sainthood, his authority redirected into lineage, and his voice absorbed into institutional memory. Such processes did not arise to serve humanity as a whole, but to secure religious ownership and doctrinal continuity.

Yet the truth itself could not be erased. The radiance of his words and the clarity of his vision endured—truth expressed without hierarchy, devotion without exclusion, and humanity affirmed as divine. Preserved in living speech, his message resisted later alteration; language itself became a vessel guarding a teaching grounded in equality, compassion, and oneness.

Beyond the shifting Bhaktmāl narratives and theological constructions, an enduring reality emerges. Ravidass appears not merely as a seeker moving toward the Divine, but as a presence through whom the Divine was encountered—walking among the humble, speaking in the language of lived truth, and restoring faith not in distant heavens, but in the sacred dignity of human life.

Glory of Ravidass
&
Bhaktamal

Chapter Thirteen

The Path of Divine Realism

Ravidass articulated a path through which devotion is realized while fully engaged in the world. His teaching affirms that true spirituality does not require withdrawal from life, but awakening within it. For his followers, the Divine is not distant, but present and accessible.

At a time when many seekers renounced household life for forests and ascetic practice, Ravidass demonstrated that liberation may be discovered amid daily labor itself. He continued in his ancestral occupation, transforming it into a spiritual discipline—stitching torn leather outwardly while inwardly guiding souls toward Hari, the Eternal. Through this lived example, he affirmed that spiritual realization does not abandon the responsibilities of life but fulfills them with integrity and devotion. In doing so, he challenged social hierarchies and declared that no occupation is low when performed in remembrance of the Divine. The true temple, he taught, is formed within the heart through Naam Simran.

In his household life as well, he stood as an example of integrity. Tradition remembers Mata Lona as his devoted companion, and their son Vijay Dass within a continuing lineage. In Banaras, descendants associated with his family remain part of living memory. Yet his enduring legacy lies not in bloodline, but in spiritual inheritance—in the transmission of remembrance, humility, and equality.

Ravidass consistently emphasized transformation of the inner life. The five passions—desire, anger, greed, attachment, and jealousy—are not denied but redirected toward devotion and compassion. In the Bani, these forces are described as having combined to plunder the world when left unchecked. Yet, through remembrance and the grace of the Guru, they are transformed into the very means of awakening. In this way, his teaching embodies a form of divine realism: the sacred discovered not apart from the world, but within it.

Jan Ravidass Rām rang rātā.
Iu gur parsād narak nahī jātā.

Ravidass declares: dyed in the Love of the Lord, through the Guru's Grace one does not fall into darkness.

In this vision, the path revealed by Ravidass was never meant for one alone. The grace he realized flowed through the fellowship of the *sangat,* where the praises of the Divine were sung beyond attachment to any single name or form. Within this living current, seekers were transformed—not by lineage or privilege, but through the awakening of devotion (*Bhagti*) and the grace of the Guru.

Thus, the path of Ravidass endures not as inheritance, but as realization—carried in the hearts of those who remember the Divine.

Where remembrance awakens, the world itself becomes the path, and the One is found already present within.

Chapter Fourteen

Jhali

Life and Royal Lineage

Rani Ratan Jhali of Mewar was the queen consort of Rana Raimal (r. 1473–1509 CE) and the mother of Rana Sanga (r. 1509–1528 CE), two renowned rulers of the Sisodia dynasty. She lived during a transformative era in North Indian history, when the current of bhakti devotion flowed beyond temples and courts, softening rigid social boundaries and awakening spiritual inquiry across regions.

The royal court of Mewar, long celebrated for valor and dharma, became in this period not only a center of political strength but also a space receptive to devotional movements that emphasized humility, equality, and remembrance of the Divine.

Receiving Satnam Amrit from Ravidass

In Bhaktmal (1585 CE), Nabha Das records Rani Jhali among the noble devotees associated with Ravidass. This early testimony is significant, as it predates later commentarial expansions and reflects an early devotional memory preserved within the Bhakti tradition. Certain early printed recensions recount that after performing Ganga Ishnan, Rani Jhali traveled to Kāshi for the darshan of Ravidass. By that time, his renown had spread widely, and he was honored in Kashi as Satguru Ravidass, whose presence embodied the Light of Hari. Drawn by his teaching of oneness and the equality of all souls, the Queen accepted him as her Guru and received Satnam Amrit in his presence.

The Bhaktmal further suggests that his fame extended across Bharat, attracting seekers from diverse regions — saints, scholars, and householders alike — who came to hear the wisdom that transcended caste and ritual boundaries.

The Royal Langar of Equality

Bhakti tradition further preserves an episode associated with Rani Jhali's devotion in Mewar. At her invitation, Ravidass and members of his sangat are said to have visited the royal court. A grand langar was arranged, and saints, scholars, and Brahmin pandits were invited to partake together.

Some among the learned guests, conditioned by prevailing social customs, hesitated to dine alongside devotees of humble background. Seeing their reluctance, the Queen is described as troubled. Ravidass, however, is remembered as responding with calm assurance:

"Let them eat first."

According to later devotional accounts, as the pandits began their meal, each perceived Ravidass seated beside him — and yet he was simultaneously seen among the gathered sangat. Astonished, they reported to the Queen that though there was one Ravidass, each experienced his presence personally.

Within the symbolic language of Bhakti hagiography, this moment signified a profound realization: the Divine Light cannot be confined to one body, one caste, or one rank. Pride dissolved into humility. The external markers of distinction lost their meaning before the experience of spiritual equality.

As related in later commentarial traditions associated with , the episode concludes with Ravidass affirming that distinctions of birth and status fade before the One Light present in all.

Whether read as miracle narrative or devotional allegory, the royal langar of Mewar stands as a powerful illustration of his message — that the Divine makes no distinction among souls.

In that royal court, the feast became more than a meal — it became a revelation that the true langar of the Divine is shared humanity itself.

Chapter Fifteen

Pipa

The Life of a King Who Found God

Raja Pipa, born in 1425 CE at Gagron Fort in present-day Rajasthan, belonged to a noble Rajput lineage. From youth he displayed both royal valor and inward spiritual inclination.

Ascending the throne, he ruled with justice and dignity. Yet devotional memory portrays him as increasingly aware of the impermanence of worldly authority. In time, he renounced royal wealth and embraced the path of bhakti.

Leaving behind the fortress of kingship, he joined the fellowship of saints and adopted the life of a seeker. His life stands as a symbol: temporal crowns fade, but the sovereignty of inner realization endures.

His hymn, preserved in the Adi Granth, reflect humility, surrender, and longing for the Divine. They emphasize interior realization over ritual observance and proclaim Naam as the true treasure beyond all worldly wealth.

He lived within the wider Sant milieu of the fifteenth century, alongside figures such as Ravidass, whose teachings likewise emphasized equality and direct experience of the Divine.

The Question of Discipleship

Later Vaishnava traditions identify Pipa as a disciple of Ramananda. However, in the earliest recension of Bhaktmal, the structure of the text does not explicitly establish a fixed guru–disciple lineage between Ramanand and Pipa in the systematic manner found in later sectarian literature.

The disciple lists associated with Ramanand appear more fully developed in subsequent commentarial traditions, particularly in the Parcai-s attributed to Anantadas and later redactions. These expansions reflect the process by which devotional communities organized spiritual genealogies over time.

Given the fluid nature of early Sant fellowship, it may be historically more accurate to understand Pipa as part of a shared devotional network rather than as exclusively bound within a later institutional lineage.

Notably, Rajasthan preserves abundant oral traditions associated with Ravidass, suggesting that his devotional current had already extended westward during the fifteenth century.

Bhaktmal Commentaries (16th–20th Century): Narrative Development and Lineage Formation

In later Bhaktiras ṭikas, Raja Pipa is described as traveling to Kashi in search of Ramananda. In one account, Ramanand tests him by instructing him to leap into a well for the darshan of Hari. When Pipa hesitates, he is told to return after deepening his devotion. In subsequent retellings, Pipa is said to return again to Kashi, meet Kabir, and escort him and his Guru to Gagron Fort in Rajasthan, where initiation and communal fellowship follow.

These narratives appear more fully in the expanded devotional literature associated with Anantadas and later commentarial traditions. They reflect the gradual process by which spiritual communities articulated structured guru–disciple relationships within emerging Vaishnava frameworks.

The Rajasthan Oral Sakhi

In contrast, Rajasthan's living oral Sakhi tradition preserves a different emphasis. In these accounts, Raja Pipa approaches Ravidass in humility, concealing his royal identity beneath a shawl. In one widely narrated episode, he mistakenly pours the sacred Amrit into the sleeve (Jamal) of his robe rather than drinking it — a symbolic moment of spiritual immaturity followed by repentance and renewed devotion. Moved by sincerity, Ravidass blesses him with true Naam Amrit.

Whether read literally or allegorically, the Sakhi conveys a central Sant theme: humility precedes realization, and grace perfects devotion.

Chronology and Textual Development

Several historical reconstructions place Ramananda in the late fourteenth to early fifteenth century (commonly c. 1299–1410 CE, though alternative datings exist). If Raja Pipa's birth is accepted as 1425 CE, as preserved in regional records of Rajasthan, direct discipleship becomes historically complex under that chronological framework.

Furthermore, the earliest recension of Bhaktmal does not present fully systematized guru–disciple hierarchies in the structured manner seen in later Vaishnava commentaries. More elaborate lineage constructions appear progressively in the traditions associated with Anantadas and later redactors such as Priyadas.

This layered evolution suggests that devotional memory developed across generations, gradually formalizing relationships that may originally have existed within a more fluid Sant fellowship.

HISTORICAL CONSIDERATIONS

Three observations emerge from comparative reading:

Chronological Tension

Under the commonly accepted dating of Ramanand's life, chronological overlap with a Pipa born in 1425 CE requires careful examination.

Textual Layering

The earliest Bhaktmal layer offers concise devotional references rather than fully articulated lineage systems; later commentaries increasingly organize saints within hierarchical Vaishnava structures.

Regional Continuity

Rajasthan preserves independent oral traditions linking Pipa with Ravidass, indicating that multiple streams of devotional memory coexisted before later consolidation.

Concluding Reflection

Rather than viewing these differences as contradiction, they may be understood as evidence of historical development. The Sant milieu of the fifteenth century appears to have been interconnected and dynamic, not yet confined within rigid institutional boundaries.

Within that broader devotional fellowship, Raja Pipa's hymns — preserved in the Adi Granth — resonate strongly with themes associated with Ravidass: humility, interior realization, and equality beyond caste and ritual.

Chronology and textual history together invite thoughtful reconsideration of later lineage attributions, while honoring the complexity of devotional transmission across centuries.

Chapter Sixteen

Dhanna

The Devotion of the Humble Farmer

Dhanna is traditionally dated to 1415 CE, with regional records placing his birth in the village of Dhuan Kalan in present-day Rajasthan. Born to Bhai Panna and Mata Reva, he grew up within a modest agrarian household. From childhood, he is remembered for his tenderness toward animals and deep reverence for the land.

As he matured, Dhanna married Sundari Bai and established a household. Yet even while fulfilling worldly responsibilities, his heart remained fixed upon the Divine. While plowing his fields or tending cattle, he experienced the presence of Hari in the rhythm of daily labor.

Bhakti tradition records that Dhanna journeyed to Kashi, where he entered the fellowship of saints and received initiation into the remembrance of Naam. Though later sources vary in identifying his initiating Guru, his hymns consistently emphasize interior devotion over ritual observance.

From that point forward, farming itself became his worship. The plow became his instrument of meditation; the fields, his temple. In seed and rain, in cattle and harvest, he perceived the One Presence.

Dhanna spent the remainder of his life in devotion, seva, and simran. His hymns, preserved in the Adi Granth, reflect simplicity and spiritual depth — affirming that the Divine is accessible not through status or scholarship, but through sincerity of heart.

He is remembered as having left his earthly form in Rajasthan, but his legacy endures: the farmer-saint who showed that remembrance transforms labor into prayer and humility into spiritual sovereignty.

Bhaktmal Commentary

Devotion in Simplicity

In the commentarial traditions associated with Bhaktmal and its later ṭīkās, Dhanna is remembered as the embodiment of rural simplicity and sincere devotion. His life, though outwardly ordinary, became luminous in devotional memory.

One widely preserved account narrates that while working in his fields, Dhanna encountered a group of traveling saints. Greeting them with folded hands, he listened as they spoke of the Lord and the sweetness of remembrance. Moved by their words, he humbly requested (jodrī) that they bless his home with their presence. Recognizing his sincerity, the saints accepted.

Dhanna prepared a simple meal from the grain available to him — even using seed meant for sowing. Each act of service, from drawing water to placing food before his guests, is described as filled with reverence. Pleased by his devotion, the saints blessed him and encouraged him to remain steadfast in the path of Naam.

Later devotional expansions recount that because Dhanna had offered his seed grain in service, the Lord Himself tended his fields. Whether read literally or symbolically, the narrative expresses a core Bhakti teaching: when devotion becomes complete, worldly anxiety dissolves.

A Shared Pattern in Bhakti Memory

Across the broader Bhakti landscape, similar turning points are preserved in the lives of saints such as Beni, Bhikhan, and Surdas. In each case, devotional memory emphasizes an inward awakening — a moment when pride, learning, or ritual certainty yielded to humility and surrender.

Although detailed early biographies remain limited, their spiritual authority endures through their bani preserved in the Adi Granth. Together, these lives affirm a shared Sant insight: one genuine encounter with realized truth can redirect an entire life toward the Eterna

The Miracle of the Blooming Fields

Devotional tradition further recounts that after Dhanna journeyed to Kashi (Banaras) to deepen his spiritual practice and serve his Satguru, a remarkable event occurred in his native village of Dhuan Kalan.

Villagers later reported seeing Dhanna in his fields — ploughing, sowing, and tending the land as before. The crops grew tall and golden under the sun, and the harvest prospered. Yet when Dhanna eventually returned, he was astonished to find his fields flourishing despite his long absence.

According to Bhakti memory, the villagers insisted they had seen him working daily. Dhanna, moved to tears, bowed in gratitude and recognized the event as divine grace. Within the symbolic language of Sant tradition, the story affirms a central conviction: the Lord sustains the labor of those who serve with sincerity.

His hymns, preserved in the Adi Granth, echo this spirit of dependence upon the Divine — expressing that human effort alone does not bear fruit without the sustaining Presence.

Whether read literally or devotionally, the blooming fields of Dhanna stand as an enduring metaphor: when the heart is surrendered, even ordinary labor becomes sustained by unseen grace.

Historical Clarification

Modern scholarship has revisited many of the hagiographical associations found in later Bhaktmal commentaries. Winand M. Callewaert, in collaboration with Dr. Swapna Sharma in The Hagiographies of Anantadas, notes that P. Caturvedi identified one of the earliest references linking Dhanna and Ramanand in a verse attributed to Mira. However, Caturvedi observes that the verse is purely encomiastic and does not provide reliable historical evidence of formal discipleship. He further situates Dhanna chronologically after Ravidass and concludes that Dhanna's association with Ramanand is historically uncertain.

Chronological analysis reinforces this assessment. Dhanna is traditionally dated to 1415 CE in Dhuan Kalan (Rajasthan), while several historical reconstructions place Ramananda's death around 1410 CE (though alternate datings exist). Under this widely accepted framework, direct discipleship becomes historically difficult.

By contrast, later commentaries — including that of Priyadas (1712 CE) — present more systematized lineage structures, grouping Dhanna, Sain, Kabir, and others within Ramanandi succession. Such developments reflect the evolving theological organization of Bhakti communities across the seventeenth and eighteenth centuries.

These layered textual traditions demonstrate how devotional memory gradually took institutional form over time.

Concluding Reflection

Whether through village fields in Rajasthan or the spiritual gatherings of Kashi, Dhanna's story preserves a central Sant insight: the Divine is not confined to ritual, rank, or institution, but is encountered in sincerity of heart.

His hymns, preserved in the Adi Granth, affirm the equality of all before the One. In them, labor becomes devotion, humility becomes strength, and remembrance becomes the true path.

Rather than viewing later lineage attributions as contradiction, they may be understood as part of the historical evolution of Bhakti traditions. Yet Dhanna's own voice remains clear — centered on Naam, simplicity, and trust in the sustaining Presence.

In that enduring testimony, the original light of devotion continues to shine — not bound by chronology or sect, but carried forward in living remembrance.

Chapter Seventeen

Mira

The Royal Devotee of Divine Love

Mirabai, one of the most luminous figures of the Bhakti movement, was born in 1498 CE at Kudki near Pali in Rajasthan, to Rao Ratan Singh Rathore. She was later married to Rana Bhojraj, crown prince of Mewar. Yet even within royal life, her devotion was directed solely toward her chosen Lord, whom she called Giridhar.

It is generally believed that Mira left her earthly form around 1547 CE. Her bhajans — simple, ecstatic, and overflowing with longing — remain among the enduring treasures of India's devotional literature.

Her Life Within the Sant Milieu

By the late fifteenth and early sixteenth century, Kashi (Banaras) had become a vibrant center of Sant spirituality. The teachings associated with figures such as Ravidass, Kabir, and Sain circulated widely across North India, including Rajasthan.

Within certain devotional traditions, particularly those preserved in Mewar and among Ravidass-centered communities, Mira Bai is remembered as having come into contact with the spiritual current associated with Ravidass. Through the influence of Rani Ratan

Jhali of Mewar, she is said to have heard of his teachings and to have sought deeper initiation into Naam.

These traditions recount that Mira received guidance and blessing from Ravidass, embracing a form of devotion that transcended caste, gender, and courtly expectation. In her poetry, she addresses her Lord as Giridhar, Govind, and Hari — names that reflect both Vaishnava imagery and the broader Sant emphasis on direct, personal experience of the Divine.

Mira Bai's Bhakti and Bani

Mirabai did not compose a formal scripture during her lifetime. Her devotional songs circulated orally among communities of singers and devotees before being collected in later manuscripts. With her ektara in hand, she sang verses of longing and surrender, addressing her Lord through names such as Giridhar, Govind, Hari, and Krishna.

Her poetry was later compiled in various regional recensions. In the twentieth century, P. Chaturvedi edited one influential collection titled Mīrābāī kī Padāvalī, preserving many verses attributed to her within the living devotional tradition.

Among these recensions, certain verses explicitly mention Ravidass as Guru. For example:

Satgur miliya saansa bhagya, Sain batai saanchi.
Guru Ravidass mile mohin pūre, dhur se kalam bhīṛī.
Satguru Sain daī jab chāke, jot main jot raī.

In translation, these lines express themes of spiritual transformation:

"When I met the True Guru, my doubts vanished; He showed me the path of truth."
"When I met Guru Ravidass, my destiny was inscribed anew from its origin."
"When the True Guru revealed the truth, my light merged into the Divine Light."

While the manuscript history of these verses is complex and debated, their presence in several devotional traditions reflects a remembered association between Mira and the Sant lineage linked to Ravidass.

In that remembered fellowship, Mira emerges not merely as a royal devotee, but as a voice of fearless devotion — one who challenged social constraint through unwavering love of the Divine. Whether through courtly halls or temple gatherings, her songs carried forward the flame of Bhakti across generations.

Popular Stories of Devotion and Trial

Later devotional traditions recount that after Mira's deepening association with Sant spirituality, her intense and public devotion created tension within the royal household of Mewar. Her unwavering singing, temple visits, and disregard for courtly expectations challenged prevailing norms.

One widely preserved narrative tells that a cup of poison was sent to her, disguised as Charan Amrit. Some versions attribute this act to members of the royal family unsettled by her spiritual independence. Mira is said to have accepted the cup without fear, declaring that if it came in the name of her Lord or Guru, it could bring no harm. According to devotional memory, the poison became nectar, and she remained unharmed.

Another popular story recounts that a basket containing a cobra was sent to test her faith. When she opened it, she found instead a garland of flowers. Such accounts, whether read literally or symbolically, portray Mira's absolute surrender — a faith that transformed danger into grace.

After the death of her husband, Rana Bhojraj (d. 1521 CE), Mira's position within the royal court became increasingly precarious. Later retellings associate opposition with figures such as Rana Vikramaditya. The historical details vary across sources, but the devotional tradition consistently emphasizes her refusal to abandon her path of bhakti.

In these narratives, Mira responds not with resentment but humility:

> *"Do not seek forgiveness from me. Ask it from the Lord—for He alone protects."*

Whether understood as miracle or metaphor, these stories express a central Bhakti conviction: unwavering devotion transcends worldly power, and surrender dissolves fear.

Mira and Classical Ragas

Mirabai's bhajans, though originally transmitted orally, came to be sung within classical raga frameworks in later devotional traditions. In her poetry, music becomes an instrument of surrender — sound itself a pathway to the Divine. For Mira, melody was not performance but worship; each raga carried longing toward Hari.

Certain devotional streams associated with Ravidass emphasize that Sant spirituality in Kashi deeply influenced regional bhakti currents across North India. Within those traditions, Mira's devotion is remembered as resonating with the Sant emphasis on Naam and interior realization.

Mira Bai's Bani and Scriptural Preservation

The preservation of Mirabai's verses presents a complex textual history. Much of her bani circulated orally for generations before being gathered into regional recensions. As a result, variations and interpolations emerged over time, reflecting the fluid character of living devotional transmission.

Certain early manuscript traditions connected with Sant literature — including manuscript environments in which the Adi Granth circulated — contain noteworthy marginal or sectional references. In some manuscript evidence, a notation under Rāg Māru identifies a section as "Bani Mira Bai Ji Ki," appearing before Rāg Tukhāri. While such references are not present in later standardized printed editions, their manuscript occurrence suggests that verses attributed to Mira were known within circles that also preserved Sant compositions.

By the fifteenth century, regional Punjabi script forms — ancestral to later standardized Gurmukhi — were already in use in administrative, mercantile, and devotional settings. The eventual preservation of Sant bani in standardized Gurmukhi manuscripts reflects not the sudden creation of script, but the formalization of an existing written culture that had long supported vernacular devotional expression.

Devotion Over Fire

In an age when widowhood in royal Rajasthan stood beneath the shadow of Sati, Mira chose another fire — the fire of devotion.

After the death of Rana Bhojraj, she refused to surrender her life to custom and instead surrendered it wholly to the Divine.

In that choice, she transformed fear into faith and widowhood into freedom. Her defiance was not rebellion for power, but surrender to love — a love no court could command and no flame could consume.

Ravidass Charan Paduka and the Mira Bai Temple

According to long-standing devotional tradition at Chittorgarh, Ravidass transcended to the celestial realm in 1527 CE (1584 Vikram Samvat). It is remembered that at the time of his departure, he did not leave behind a physical body, but only his Charan Paduka — sacred footprints that came to be revered by generations of devotees.

At Chittorgarh Fort today stands a shrine commonly known as the Mira Bai Temple complex, where a site dedicated to Ravidass is also venerated. Local tradition holds that Mira, in remembrance of her Satguru, honored this sacred place. Whether through direct patronage or later devotional continuity, the association reflects the enduring spiritual bond remembered between Mira and Ravidass.

The Charan Paduka serve not merely as relics but as symbols—the path walked by Ravidass and the path offered to seekers. In living memory, Mira's reverence for her Guru carried a message beyond sect or creed: the Divine belongs to no single community; the Light dwells in every heart.

Essence

Mira's devotion is not merely verse but surrender given voice. Her life embodies a Sant conviction echoed across the fifteenth century—that divine love dissolves hierarchy, remembrance overcomes fear, and the light within the disciple seeks its home in the Light of the Guru.

Chapter Eighteen

Sain

The Saint of Humble Service

Sain is generally dated to around 1400 CE and is traditionally associated with the Punjab region, with later accounts placing his birth in Sohal (in present-day Tarn Taran district). While early biographical details vary across sources, devotional tradition consistently situates him within the early fifteenth-century Sant milieu.

Though humble by profession, Sain became known as a luminous voice of devotion. Drawn to the spiritual ferment of Kashi, he joined the fellowship of saints who emphasized Naam, humility, and service over ritual and rank.

Within certain traditions, Sain is remembered as having associated closely with Ravidass. His bani, preserved in the Adi Granth, affirms that true greatness lies not in worldly status but in surrender and remembrance of the Divine.

Later Bhaktmal commentaries include Sain among the revered saints of the age, demonstrating the enduring respect for his spiritual legacy. Devotional memory places his final years in Kashi, where he is said to have merged into the Eternal Light.

Bhaktmals Commentary

In the commentary of Priyadas (1712 CE), Sain is described as residing in the Punjab region (often identified with Taran Taran) and hosting a group of saints in his home. Moved by their spiritual presence, he served them with devotion. Upon learning that they had journeyed from Kashi — the great center of Sant spirituality — Sain is said to have traveled there himself. In this recension, Priyadas associates him with Ramananda.

By contrast, the earlier tradition attributed to Anantadas presents a different emphasis. In that account, Sain is already depicted in Kashi within the devotional environment that includes figures such as Ravidass, Kabir, and Dhanna. Rather than constructing a formal lineage, this earlier layer situates Sain within a shared Sant fellowship centered on Naam and humility.

The variation between these accounts illustrates the gradual formation of structured guru–disciple genealogies in later Bhaktmal commentaries. Earlier narratives appear less concerned with institutional affiliation and more focused on devotional association within a broader spiritual milieu.

The Devotional Tale

A cherished narrative preserved in later Bhaktmal traditions recounts that one evening, while Saint Sain was absorbed in serving visiting sadhus with complete devotion, he neglected his duty at the royal palace, where he worked as a vaid (Ayurvedic healer). The saints had arrived as guests, and kirtan continued through the night. Bound by love for the holy company, Sain did not leave their presence.

The following morning, when he appeared before the king, he expected reprimand. Instead, the ruler greeted him with astonishment:

"But you came last night and treated my wound."

In that moment, devotional memory tells us, Sain realized that the Divine had fulfilled his worldly obligation in his stead. Whether understood literally or symbolically, the story conveys a central Sant conviction: that sincere devotion does not conflict with duty, and that the Lord sustains those who surrender themselves in truth.

A concise version of this episode appears in Vār 10 of Bhai Gurdas, indicating that the narrative was already circulating within early Sikh and Bhakti communities:

Sun paratāp Kabīr dā dūjā sikh hoā Sain nāī.
Prem bhagat rātī karai, bhalke rāj duārai jāī.
Sain rūp Har hoi kai āiā, rāṇe nõ rījhāī.

Hearing the glory of Kabir, Sain the barber became the second disciple.
Immersed in loving devotion by night, he served at the royal court by day.
The Lord Himself came in the form of Sain and pleased the king.

The presence of this account in Bhai Gurdas's Vārs — composed in the late sixteenth to early seventeenth century — suggests that Sain's devotion was remembered not as isolated legend, but as part of the living spiritual memory of the Bhakti fellowship. The story does not elevate Sain through miracle alone; it reveals the Sant teaching that when ego dissolves, divine grace becomes active in the life of the devotee.

Thus, Saint Sain's life stands as a testament to humility in action: service to saints by night, service to society by day — and in both, remembrance of the One.

Historical Clarification

The testimony preserved in the Vārās of Bhai Gurdas, composed in the late sixteenth and early seventeenth centuries, occupies an important place in early Sikh exegetical tradition. Guru Arjan Dev is remembered as having described Bhai Gurdas's writings as a "key" to understanding the Adi Granth, highlighting their interpretive significance within the Guru–Bhagat framework.

When these early sources are compared with later hagiographical accounts attributed to Anantadas and Priyadas, chronological questions arise. Saint Sain is generally placed between c. 1400–1490 CE. Several historical reconstructions situate Ramananda's death around 1410 CE. If this framework is accepted, Sain would have been a child at the time of Ramanand's passing, making direct discipleship historically difficult.

The Vārs of Bhai Gurdas, composed more than a century before Priyadas's commentary, associate Sain within a devotional fellowship that includes Kabir and other Sant figures. They do not explicitly construct a formal Ramanandi lineage. It is also important to distinguish Bhai Gurdas from a later eighteenth-century writer of similar name.

Taken together, these textual layers suggest that earlier traditions emphasized shared spiritual fellowship in Kashi, while later commentaries increasingly organized saints within structured genealogies. Such developments reflect the historical evolution of Bhakti communities rather than a single fixed lineage.

Broader Context

The convergence of these traditions invites reflection. The fifteenth century witnessed an extraordinary flowering of Sant spirituality in Kashi, where figures such as Kabir, Sain, Dhanna, and Ravidass moved within overlapping devotional circles. Rather than rigid hierarchies, early sources suggest a shared fellowship centered on Naam, humility, and direct experience of the Divine.

Within devotional memory, Ravidass appears as a central presence in this Sant milieu — a teacher whose message of equality and compassion resonated across regions from Rajasthan to Punjab. Movement between Kashi and their native lands fostered a vibrant exchange of song, language, and devotion.

By the fifteenth century, regional Punjabi script forms were already in circulation. The later standardization of Gurmukhi manuscripts reflects an effort to preserve vernacular sacred utterance with phonetic clarity. While direct causal links remain debated, Sant devotional networks helped create a culture in which spoken revelation increasingly sought written preservation.

The Bhakti Roots of Classical Music

Indian classical music did not arise solely within imperial courts. Long before the refinement of Dhrupad under Mughal patronage, devotional singing flourished among poet-singers such as Mira, Kabir, and Sain, who carried sacred verse through melody across villages and royal centers alike.

The path walked by Ravidass became the path offered to seekers. In living memory, Mira's reverence for her Guru carried a message beyond sect or creed: the Divine belongs to no single community; the Light dwells in every heart.

The great master Swami Haridas (c.1480–1575) embodied the meeting of Bhakti devotion and classical discipline, and his disciple Tansen later carried this depth into the Mughal court. Courtly refinement and devotional fervor thus evolved in dialogue rather than opposition.

In that shared musical world, Mira's singing stands as devotion made sound—raga as prayer, melody as surrender.

Conclusion

The comparison of early and later Bhaktmāl traditions reveals how devotional memory evolved across generations. While later commentators organized figures into formal lineages, earlier sources and chronological study point instead to a fluid Sant fellowship centered in Kashi during the fifteenth century.

Within this shared spiritual milieu of Kashi, Sain reflects the same current of Naam, humility, and direct realization that flowed among the seekers of that time. What emerges is not rigid hierarchy but a fellowship bound by experience of the Divine rather than institutional structure.

Sain's legacy remains timeless: when devotion is sincere and service selfless, the Divine sustains the devotee. In that faith, humility becomes strength, and the servant becomes luminous with grace.

Chapter Nineteen

Sadhna

A Voice from the Early Sant Tradition

Sadhna is traditionally dated to the late twelfth and early thirteenth centuries and associated with Sehwan in Sindh (now in present-day Pakistan). Devotional memory portrays him as contemplative from youth, inclined toward the Eternal despite humble circumstances.

His bani, preserved in the Adi Granth, reflects a voice marked by detachment, humility, and surrender. The hymn attributed to him expresses a soul that has moved beyond pride and possession into reliance upon the Divine alone.

Interestingly, the name of Sadhna appears in the bani of Ravidass, alongside other earlier saints such as Namdev and Trilochan. This cross-generational remembrance suggests the continuity of Sant memory across centuries. Whether through oral transmission or spiritual reverence, the invocation of earlier saints reflects a devotional unity that transcended time and geography.

Sadhna is remembered as having left his earthly life in the thirteenth century, yet his voice endures through the scripture that preserves his hymn — a testament to the enduring fellowship of the saints.

In this way, the voice of Sadhna stands among the early currents that would later blossom more visibly in the Sant tradition. Though centuries separate these figures, the same spirit of surrender and remembrance flows through them all, carried forward in the living current of the Divine Word.

Chapter Twenty

Sheikh Farid

The Sufi Voice of Early Punjabi Devotion

Sheikh Farid, lovingly known as Baba Farid Ganjshakar ("Treasure of Sweetness"), is traditionally dated to 1173–1265 CE. He is associated with the Multan region of Punjab (now in present-day Pakistan) and belonged to the Chishti Sufi order, being the son of Sheikh Jamal-ud-Din Suleiman and Bibi Qarsum.

His verses, composed in early Punjabi, reflect deep renunciation, remembrance of the Divine, and humility before the Creator. Circulating initially through oral transmission within Sufi networks, several of his shabads were later preserved in the Adi Granth. In that scripture his voice appears among the earliest recorded expressions of devotional poetry in the region.

Farid's bani emphasizes detachment from worldly pride, constant remembrance, and the equality of all before God — themes that resonate strongly with later Sant and Bhakti traditions.

Among the Saloks preserved in the Ādi Granth are the following verses:

Farīdā je tū akal latīf, kāle likh na lekh.
Āpnṛe girīvān meh, sir nīvā kar dekh.

Farid turns the seeker inward. Wisdom lies not in judging others but in examining one's own heart; devotion begins in humility.

Kāgā karang dhandoliā, saglā khāiā mās.
E dui nainā mat chhuho, pir dekhan kī ās.

Through stark imagery, Farid reveals the impermanence of the body. All that belongs to the world fades, yet the eyes remain sacred—still longing for the Beloved.

In these brief verses, the voice of early Punjabi devotion speaks with clarity—beyond sect or identity, grounded in humility, remembrance, and love.

He is traditionally believed to have left his earthly body in 1265 CE. His shrine at Pakpattan remains a place of remembrance, reflecting the meeting of Sufi and Sant devotional currents in early Punjab.

Through these verses his voice continues across centuries. Preserved within the Ādi Granth, they reveal a longing for the One that transcends boundaries and flows into the shared spiritual heritage of the region.

Chapter Twenty-one

Maharishi Valmiki

The Seer of Transformation

Valmiki, revered as the Ādi Kavi — the first poet — composed the Valmiki Ramayana, the great Sanskrit epic traditionally situated in the age of Tretā Yuga, narrating the exile of Rama, the abduction of Sita, and the triumph of dharma over adharma. In later devotional traditions, Rama and Sita are honored as divine manifestations restoring harmony to the world.

Within the epic's unfolding — from the forest exile to the war in Lanka — the story becomes a meditation on righteousness, loyalty, suffering, and ultimate victory. Festivals such as Dussehra and Dipavali continue to commemorate these sacred memories in living tradition.

Yet Valmiki himself embodies an even deeper transformation. Tradition remembers him not as born a sage, but as one who awakened through the power of sacred utterance. Through realization, he became the seer of divine truth.

It is this transformation that Ravidass invokes in his bani, gently questioning those who measure worth by birth:

"Why do you not recognize Valmiki, who attained the Lord through Naam?"

In recalling Valmiki, Ravidass affirms a central Sant teaching: realization is not inherited — it is awakened. The light of Naam can elevate any soul, and the one once overlooked may become the voice of eternal wisdom.

Chapter Twenty-two

Krishna

Krishna is revered across devotional traditions as an avatāra of Vishnu, remembered for restoring dharma and guiding humanity through love, wisdom, and courage. According to classical tradition, he appeared in the Dvāpara Yuga to reestablish moral and spiritual balance in an age of decline.

He is universally honored as the teacher of the Bhagavad Gita — a dialogue that addresses duty, action, detachment, and devotion. Through this teaching, Krishna emerges as a guide who brings clarity to the struggles of human life, revealing how righteousness may be upheld even amid conflict.

In his youth, Krishna studied under Sandipani Muni, reflecting the sacred discipline of the guru–shishya tradition. His friendship with Sudama remains a cherished example of grace without pride and love beyond wealth.

The murli (flute) associated with Krishna has become a symbol of Bhakti spirituality — representing the Divine call that draws the soul inward. In devotional thought, harmony arises when ego falls silent and the heart responds to that subtle music.

Tradition further describes Krishna as embodying sixteen kalās, signifying completeness and fullness of divine qualities. Yet beyond attributes and theology, he is remembered most deeply as the Lord of love — one whose presence protects the righteous and invites the soul into devotion.

Krishna in the Bhagavad Gita

In the Bhagavad Gita (10.31), Krishna speaks in symbolic language, identifying himself with the most exalted manifestations within creation:

"Of rivers, I am the Ganga."

These declarations form part of the Vibhūti Yoga (Chapter 10), in which Krishna reveals his presence through the highest, most sustaining, and most luminous realities of the world. Such statements are widely understood not as claims of literal exclusivity, but as metaphysical affirmation—that the Divine pervades, sustains, and animates all that nourishes and purifies life.

Krishna and Sudama

A devotional remembrance of the meeting between Krishna and Sudama appears in Vār 10 of Bhai Gurdas. The account highlights not royal splendor, but humility, affection, and reverence grounded in shared discipleship.

Bhai Gurdas writes:

Bip Sudāmā dāldī bāl sakhāī mitar sadāe.
Dūrohũ dekh daṇḍaut kar chhaḍ siṅghāsan Har jī āe.
Puchhe kusal piār kar gur sevā dī kathā suṇāe.

Sudama, the humble Brahmin, was known as the Lord's
childhood companion.
Seeing him bow from afar, the Lord rose from His throne and

came forward.
With loving concern, He inquired of his well-being and listened to the account of his service to the Guru.

The emphasis of the narrative is striking. The Lord does not remain seated in majesty; He rises. He does not question status; He asks about devotion. The center of their reunion is not wealth, but gur-sevā — the shared discipline and humility formed in the gurukul of their youth.

Traditional accounts remember Krishna and Sudama as fellow students shaped by reverence for their teacher. Their meeting in Dwarka expresses a Bhakti ideal in which social distinction dissolves before sincere devotion. Honor flows toward humility, and grace follows affection unasked.

Chapter Twenty-three

Ravidass

Presence Revealed

From a scriptural and historical perspective, Ravidass is remembered as one in whom the qualities attributed to the Divine were profoundly recognized. In the vision reflected within the Adi Granth, God is not confined to form, lineage, or title, but discerned through presence — pervading all, sustaining all, and revealed through truth, compassion, and remembrance. These same attributes resound through Ravidass's life and bani.

He spoke of "Har" not as a distant name, but as living reality — the All-pervading One present wherever remembrance is sincere. His teaching dissolves boundaries of caste, gender, and rank. Those drawn to him addressed the One through the names closest to their understanding — Ram, Allah, Narayan, Krishna — yet the Truth remained indivisible.

He did not gather followers through command; he drew seekers through recognition. In him, devotion appears as realized wholeness — not institutional authority, but completeness of experience. Devotional language sometimes describes such fullness symbolically as sixteen kalās; yet in Ravidass this completeness is expressed not through cosmic spectacle, but through fearless equality and compassionate presence.

Ravidass in the Adi Granth

The bani of Ravidass is preserved in forty shabads within the Ādi Granth, arranged across sixteen rāgas within its sacred musical structure. His voice appears not as commentary, but as integral utterance within the revealed Word.

A striking declaration expresses this realization:

"Ravidass Thakur Ban Aī."

Here, the expression signifies realized identity—not worldly elevation, but recognition of the Divine. In the Ādi Granth, "Thakur" denotes the All-pervading One; its presence here reflects realization rather than claim.

The tone of his bani carries a distinctive authority. Many hymns speak not from supplication alone, but from realized awareness—dissolving distinctions of caste, gender, and rank. The voice does not argue for equality; it speaks from within it.

In one such utterance, Ravidass declares that even the eight supernatural powers and the ten mystical perfections lie beneath the hand, revealing a vision in which spiritual attainment itself is transcended in the presence of the Divine.

Through this realization, division loses meaning and remembrance becomes shared ground. His bani, composed in rāgas and preserved in the Ādi Granth, carries this awareness through sound and meaning—direct, inclusive, and luminous.

Those who encountered him remembered him as Satguru, not to establish a boundary, but to acknowledge awakened guidance. Reverence arose not from power imposed, but from Truth perceived.

From a historical perspective grounded in scripture, Ravidass is recognized as Lord not through later elevation or sectarian assertion, but through the qualities by which the Divine is recognized in the Ādi Granth.

Beyond Conventional Lineage

Unlike many saints whose lives were later organized into formal guru–disciple genealogies, early devotional records do not consistently situate Ravidass within a clearly defined initiation lineage. In certain recensions of the Bhaktmal, he is described not merely as a saint, but as an avatār — language that signals manifestation rather than discipleship.

Such descriptions reflect how his presence was remembered: not simply as that of a seeker progressing toward realization, but as one in whom divine awareness was directly perceived. Rather than being framed beneath a hierarchical chain, he appears in early memory as a luminous center from whom others drew inspiration.

A traditional teaching widely associated with him expresses this inward emphasis:

"Mann changa to kathoti mein Ganga"

— If the mind is pure, the Ganga flows even in a small vessel.

The teaching shifts sanctity from outer pilgrimage to inner realization. Holiness is not confined to sacred geography or ritual descent; it is awakened in the heart. In this light, discipleship becomes recognition rather than inheritance. Those who approached him — whether kings, artisans, men or women — were not drawn by institution, but by presence.

Whether approached historically or devotionally, this portrayal suggests that recognition of realized presence preceded later efforts to construct structured lineage. In these early memories, the Divine is not mediated through institutional succession, but encountered through living awareness — where purity of heart becomes the true initiation.

The Divine Voice of Ravidass Preserved in Gurmukhi

The Gurmukhi script, in which the bani of Ravidass is preserved within the Adi Granth, functions as a shared vessel for realized utterance. Through its phonetic clarity, sacred compositions were spoken, sung, and transmitted with fidelity to sound and meaning. A notable feature of the Bāṇī attributed to Ravidass is the frequent use of the form "ਕਹਿ ਰਵਿਦਾਸ" (kahi Ravidāss)—a reflective expression often rendered "Ravidass declares." In another verse preserved under Mehla 5, the Bāṇī affirms: "ਸਤਿ ਭਾਖੈ ਰਵਿਦਾਸ" (Sat bhākhai Ravidāss)—"Ravidass speaks the Truth." The script did not create revelation; it arose to preserve it.

Within this preserved tradition, the voices of Ravidass and Kabir stand not in separation but in resonance. Their utterances reflect a shared realization of Sachi Preet—true love grounded in oneness —where divisions of caste, creed, and status fall away. Ravidass turns the seeker from fear of heaven and hell toward the living truth of the Divine, where through the Guru's grace the Lord, the priceless diamond, is known as the only refuge. Kabir sharpens this insight with uncompromising clarity. Distinct in tone yet united in vision, their voices reveal one current of Divine truth.

Through Gurmukhi preservation, what was once sung in living fellowship found enduring form. Sound became script, and the current of realization continues to echo across the centuries.

Chapter Twenty-four

Kabir

Life and Legacy

Kabir is generally placed between c. 1398–1518 CE and is associated with the city of Kashi (Varanasi). Tradition remembers him as born into the household of Niru and Nima, a weaving family, and as living the life of a householder while embodying uncompromising devotion to the One. His marriage to Loi and references to his children reflect the Sant ideal that realization does not require monastic withdrawal, but may unfold within ordinary domestic life.

Kabir's bani is marked by fearless clarity. He challenged ritualism, caste exclusivity, and hollow religiosity, calling seekers instead to direct remembrance of the Divine through Naam. His language—earthy, paradoxical, and piercing—continues to awaken spiritual inquiry across communities.

Within the Adi Granth, Kabir's hymns are preserved alongside those of the Gurus and Bhagats, including Ravidass. Devotional memory places Kabir and Ravidass within the same sacred milieu of fifteenth-century Kashi, where the current of Bhakti flowed through shared fellowship. Whether in public dialogue, sung kirtan, or spiritual debate, their voices converge in affirming that the Divine is not confined to temple or mosque, but realized within the awakened heart.

Kabir is traditionally believed to have left his mortal body in 1518 CE at Maghar. His passing is remembered through the well-known account that Hindus and Muslims each claimed his remains—only to find flowers beneath the shroud, symbolizing unity beyond division. His immortal bani continues to illumine seekers with uncompromising truth and compassion.

Historical Note on the Birth of Kabir

Most modern scholars place Kabir's life between the late fourteenth and early sixteenth centuries. Researchers such as Hazari Prasad Dwivedi, Charlotte Vaudeville, David N. Lorenzen, and Purushottam Agrawal—drawing on early manuscripts, linguistic analysis, and oral traditions—generally support a birth date around 1398 CE and a passing around 1518 CE. This chronology situates him within the same broader devotional era as Ravidass, Pipa, Dhanna, and Sain, reinforcing the historical plausibility of their shared spiritual environment in North India.

Kabir in the Bhaktmals Commentaries

The life of Kabir has been remembered through layered devotional traditions. Across centuries, his story has been shaped by oral memory, poetic imagination, and theological interpretation. Early narratives emphasize divine mystery; later retellings situate him within evolving social and sectarian frameworks.

The Early Record – Anantadas's Parcāī

One of the earliest extended accounts appears in the Parcāī attributed to Anantadas (late 16th century). In this narrative, Kabir is described as being found miraculously near Lahartara Lake and raised by Niru and Nima, a humble weaving couple of Banaras. Anantadas does not explicitly describe biological parentage; rather, the emphasis rests on the mystery of appearance and divine purpose.

The symbolism is clear: Kabir's authority does not arise from lineage, but from manifestation. The story portrays him as emerging beyond conventional social identity, suggesting that Truth itself entered ordinary life in unexpected form.

Modern scholars such as Winand M. Callewaert and David N. Lorenzen have noted that these early Parcāīs evolved within vibrant oral traditions. Sung, copied, and transmitted across generations, they display variation while retaining a shared devotional core: Kabir as a realized presence transcending social origin.

The Later Interpretation – Priyadas (1712 CE)

More than a century later, Priyadas, in his Bhaktiras Bodhinī (1712 CE), presented an expanded narrative. In this version, Kabir is said to have been born to a Brahmin widow who, fearing social consequences, abandoned the infant near Lahartara, where Niru and Nima then found and raised him.

This retelling reflects a shift in emphasis. Rather than focusing on mysterious manifestation, it situates Kabir within Brahminical birth, while still preserving his association with the weaving household. Many historians interpret this as an attempt to reconcile Kabir's spiritual stature with prevailing caste sensitivities of the time.

Whether viewed as theological harmonization or social accommodation, the evolution of these narratives demonstrates how Bhakti memory adapted across centuries. Yet beneath the variations remains a consistent thread: Kabir's spiritual authority does not depend on inherited status, but on realized insight.

Kabir and Ramanand

Later Bhaktmāl commentators, especially Priyadas (1712 CE), elaborated narratives connecting Kabir with Ramanand through symbolic episodes:

The Dawn at the Ganga

Kabir, desiring initiation but conscious of caste barriers, lies upon the steps of the ghats. Ramanand unknowingly steps upon him and utters "Ram, Ram," which Kabir receives as mantra.

The Garland and the Tilak

Kabir offers a garland in devotion; Ramanand later recognizes him and formally imparts the Ram mantra.

The Dutiful Disciple

Kabir is portrayed as serving Ramanand faithfully while enduring familial hardship.

These accounts are devotional in tone and rich in symbolism. Many historians regard them as retrospective constructions designed to situate Kabir within an established Vaishnava lineage.

Chronological considerations have also shaped modern discussion. Ramanand is often placed in the late 14th to early 15th century, with some traditions recording his passing around 1410 CE. If this date is accepted, Kabir would have been very young at the time, raising questions about the historical plausibility of formal discipleship. However, other scholars propose later dates for Ramanand, making the matter far from settled.

What remains clear across traditions is that Kabir emerged within the devotional milieu of North India where multiple spiritual currents converged in Kashi. Whether framed within Ramanandi lineage or understood within a broader Sant fellowship, his authority rests not on institutional affiliation but on the power of his utterance and realization.

The Gosti Between Ravidass and Kabir

Certain devotional narratives attributed to Anantadas describe a sacred gostī — a spiritual dialogue — between Ravidass and Kabir. In these accounts, the exchange is not rivalry but inquiry. Kabir poses searching questions regarding liberation and realization; Ravidass responds with composed clarity, emphasizing direct experience of the Divine beyond outer distinction.

Such dialogues, common in Bhakti literature, function less as historical transcripts and more as theological dramatizations. They reveal how early Sant communities remembered their saints — not as competitors, but as co-participants in a shared current of realization within Kashi.

The Bhavishya Purana Reference

A much later printed recension of the Bhavishya Purana (20th century) places Ravidass in debate with Kabir and links him genealogically to Adi Shankaracharya and Ramananda. Chronologically, such associations are untenable: Shankaracharya is traditionally dated to the 8th–9th century CE, several centuries before the 15th-century Sant milieu.

Most scholars therefore regard such passages as late interpolations, reflecting efforts to situate nirgun figures within older Brahmanical genealogies. These developments illustrate how devotional memory evolves, adapting revered voices into broader theological frameworks. What endures beyond layered narrative and later interpolation is the unmistakable affinity of their voices. Across preserved hymns and remembered encounters, Ravidass and Kabir emerge not as rivals in debate, but as fellow travelers within the same current of fifteenth-century spiritual realization Their shared emphasis on direct experience, humility, and freedom from caste distinction reveals a spiritual fellowship deeper than textual genealogy.

Transformation in Later Bhaktmal Commentaries

By the time of Priyadas (1712 CE), certain earlier narratives were expanded and systematized within broader sectarian frameworks. Dialogues that once emphasized unity were sometimes recast with hierarchical elements, reflecting the growing importance of lineage structures in early modern devotional communities.

Historians note that Bhaktmāl commentaries often reveal as much about the century in which they were written as about the saints they describe. As traditions consolidated, efforts were sometimes made to align independent Sant figures with established theological orders.

Saints and Royal Memory

Bhaktmāl traditions also recall that both Kabir and Ravidass drew the attention of political authorities. The name of Sikandar Lodhi appears in later devotional memory, symbolizing how their influence extended beyond artisan communities into wider social spheres. Whether fully historical or partly symbolic, such accounts affirm a recurring Bhakti theme: spiritual authority transcends political power.

Ravidass and Kabir — Shared Sant Fellowship

Historical and devotional memory places Ravidass and Kabir within the same fifteenth-century spiritual milieu of Kashi. Their preserved bani in the Adi Granth reveals striking thematic harmony: both emphasize Naam, direct realization, and the rejection of caste-based exclusion.

Kabir repeatedly bows to the Satguru as the awakener of divine vision. Devotional readers have long seen in this reverence a reflection of the realized presence embodied by figures such as Ravidass. Whether understood as formal discipleship or spiritual fellowship, their voices resonate within the same current of fifteenth-century realization. Both challenged ritualism and social hierarchy, calling seekers toward inward awakening—their convergence resting not in lineage, but in lived experience.

Preservation Through Script

The preservation of their bani in the Adi Granth ensured that these realized utterances were transmitted in stable phonetic form. The standardized Gurmukhi script provided a vehicle through which the Sant voice entered enduring textual expression. What had once been sung in fellowship became safeguarded in written scripture.

Within his preserved hymns, Ravidass explicitly recalls fellow Saints such as Kabir and Sain by name — gestures of spiritual recognition woven into the same textual fabric. Through this preservation, their shared realization was not fragmented, but carried forward in a unified scriptural form.

The Spiritual Reality

The unity between Ravidass and Kabir is reflected in the coherence of their teachings. Both proclaimed the sovereignty of Naam, uplifted marginalized communities, and spoke of the Divine beyond sectarian boundaries. Their shared message transformed the devotional landscape of North India.

Kabir himself expresses the transformative power of the realized saint:

Kabir Pāras mein aur sant mein, bahut antarau jān.
Vah lohā kanchan kare, vah kare āpu samān.

Between the philosopher's stone and the saint there is great difference: Kabir
the stone turns iron into gold, but the saint makes another into his own likeness.

Their unity does not rest upon formal lineage, but upon shared realization. In the sacred preservation of their bani, their voices stand not in rivalry but in resonance. Where one speaks of the Formless, the other affirms its living immediacy; where one exposes illusion, the other reveals presence. Together they belong to the same current of awakening that transformed fifteenth-century Kashi — a current whose depth cannot be confined within sect or caste, and which continues to illumine the path of Naam.

Chapter Twenty-five

Jaidev

Jaidev, born in the 12th century at Kenduli (traditionally identified with Kindubilva in Bengal), was a luminous poet-saint whose devotion to Hari found expression in refined lyrical form. His poetry embodies longing (viraha), surrender, and ecstatic union — themes that shaped the devotional imagination of eastern India and beyond.

His celebrated work, Gita Govinda, remains one of the most influential compositions in the Bhakti tradition. Structured as lyrical songs to be sung in specific rāgas, it helped give sacred poetry a defined musical life. The tradition remembers an episode in which Jaidev, hesitant to write a verse describing divine intimacy, paused in humility — and the Lord Himself is said to have completed the line. Whether read symbolically or devotionally, the story reflects the poet's deep surrender before the Divine.

Two hymns attributed to Jaidev are preserved in the Adi Granth. In them, he exalts the glory of the Divine Name and the path of inward devotion. His inclusion alongside later Sant voices reflects the continuity of Bhakti across centuries. Indeed, Kabir also recalls Jaidev and Namdev in his bani, honoring them as exemplary devotees.

Saint Jaidev's life and poetry stand as early testimony that love —
refined through music, surrender, and remembrance — becomes a
path to union with the Divine.

Chapter Twenty-six

Trilochan

The Voice of Inner Detachment

Trilochan is traditionally placed in the late 13th and early 14th centuries and associated with Narsi in Maharashtra, a region that produced several early Bhakti figures. Devotional sources commonly suggest a birth around 1269 CE, though precise historical dating remains approximate.

His hymns are preserved in the Adi Granth, where they emphasize inner sincerity over external ritual. Trilochan speaks against hypocrisy and hollow ascetic display, reminding seekers that spiritual realization depends not on outward form but on remembrance of the Divine Name. His verses call for honesty, humility, and constant awareness of God in daily life.

Trilochan is closely associated with Namdev. Their shared regional background and mutual references in preserved hymns reflect a living devotional fellowship in medieval Maharashtra. In one composition, Namdev addresses Trilochan directly, suggesting familiarity and spiritual companionship.

The name of Trilochan is also mentioned by Ravidass in his bani, indicating that later Sant figures remembered earlier devotees within a continuing spiritual lineage of Naam-centered devotion.

His remembrance in Priyadas's 1712 commentary further shows how his legacy remained alive across centuries.

Tradition places Trilochan's passing around 1330 CE in Maharashtra. Whether precise dates can be confirmed or not, his preserved bani stands as enduring testimony that the truest worship lies not in appearance or renunciation, but in a heart grounded in love and remembrance of the Lord.

Chapter Twenty-seven

Namdev

The Saint of Universal Devotion

Namdev is one of the earliest and most luminous saints of medieval Bhakti. Traditionally placed around 1270–1350 CE, he is associated with Narsi in Maharashtra and later with Pandharpur, the sacred center of Vithoba devotion. Devotional sources remember him as born to Damashet (Damshet) and Gonai, and from childhood marked by deep love for the Divine.

Married to Rajai and blessed with children, Namdev embodied the Sant ideal that spiritual realization does not require monastic withdrawal. His life affirmed that devotion may flourish within household life when grounded in constant remembrance.

His devotional compositions, known as abhangs, were sung in Marathi and carried through oral tradition for centuries. These songs gave voice to the spiritual longing of ordinary people and helped shape the early Bhakti movement in western India. In modern times, they were collected in compilations such as the Sri Namdev Gatha (Government of Maharashtra edition, 1970), preserving a vast body of his attributed verses.

A selection of Namdev's hymns is preserved in the Adi Granth. Their inclusion reflects the recognition of his spiritual authority beyond regional boundaries. His bani emphasizes humility, surrender, and unwavering devotion to the Divine Name.

Later Sant figures, including Ravidass, mention Namdev in their own compositions, indicating the continued remembrance of earlier Bhakti exemplars within a broader devotional current.

Tradition places Namdev's passing around 1350 CE in Pandharpur. Whether exact dates can be verified or not, his enduring legacy lies in the simplicity and depth of his devotion — a reminder that God responds not to ritual complexity, but to the sincerity of the heart.

Anantadas's Parcai of Namdev

In the seventeenth-century Bhaktmāl tradition, Anantadas composed a Parcāī devoted to Namdev. There he presents Namdev as a luminous bhakta of the Kali age — one whose love for Hari was so intense that the Divine became visibly responsive to him.

The narrative includes episodes such as:

The feeding of the Lord;
his testing under a ruling authority;
and the well-known account of the temple turning toward the devotee.

These stories are framed not as demonstrations of personal power, but as poetic affirmations that sincere devotion renders God present and accessible. Anantadās's style reflects the devotional hagiography of his era — blending reverence, miracle, and spiritual symbolism.

Priyadas's commentary (1712 CE)

More than a century later, Priyadas composed the Bhaktiras Bodhinī ṭīkā (1712 CE), expanding and reinterpreting earlier Bhaktmāl traditions.

In this later recension, Namdev is placed within a more explicitly Vaishnava lineage; additional narrative details concerning his birth and family background are introduced; and miraculous episodes are elaborated in greater dramatic detail.

One well-known account describes young Namdev offering milk to the idol of Vithoba, which then drinks it — symbolizing the intimacy between devotee and Lord. Another narrative recounts that when denied entry to a temple, the shrine itself turned toward him in affirmation of his devotion.

Modern scholars such as Winand Callewaert, Rohini Mokashi-Punekar, and Eleanor Zelliot note that Priyādās wrote several centuries after Namdev's lifetime. His commentary reflects the theological and sectarian environment of the early eighteenth century, where saints were frequently situated within organized sampradāyas.

Rather than treating these narratives as strict biography, scholars tend to read them as devotional constructions — expressions of faith shaped by evolving community identity.

The temple episode is often associated in regional memory with the Aundha Nagnath Temple, an ancient Shaiva site. However, the precise historical setting remains uncertain, as early textual sources provide limited detail.

The Truth Preserved in Gurbani

Against evolving narrative traditions, the preserved bani of Namdev remains a stable witness. His hymns, as recorded in the Adi Granth, reject hollow ritual and caste pride, calling humanity toward inward remembrance of the Divine. His voice resonates in harmony with Ravidass and other Sant figures, affirming that God is realized not in external form but in the heart anchored in Naam.

Oral Transmission and Preservation

Namdev's abhangs circulated for centuries primarily through oral tradition. Written compilations in Marathi appear much later, including modern printed editions such as the 1970 Sri Namdev Gatha. This does not imply absence, but rather reflects the nature of early Bhakti preservation — sung, remembered, and transmitted within living communities.

The presence of Namdev's hymns in northern manuscript traditions indicates that his voice traveled far beyond Maharashtra. Devotional networks likely carried these compositions across regions long before formal compilation.

Interwoven Voices in the Adi Granth

The presence of Namdev within the Adi Granth reflects the wide circulation of his devotional voice beyond Maharashtra. His hymns, preserved alongside those of later saints, demonstrate that Bhakti was not confined to region or language but moved through living networks of remembrance.

Within the Adi Granth, certain headings reveal the layered nature of Sant transmission. Under Rāg Māru appears the attribution:

"Shabad Kabir Ji Ka, Bani Namdev Ji Ki."

Such titles do not necessarily imply editorial collaboration, but they point toward an environment in which saints invoked, echoed, and preserved one another's utterances. Their voices were not isolated; they were interwoven within a shared devotional current.

That Ravidass explicitly mentions Namdev in his own bani further suggests that earlier saints remained alive in spiritual memory. This remembrance signals continuity — not institutional lineage, but fellowship of realization.

While no extant manuscript conclusively demonstrates the original script in which Namdev first recorded his utterances, the form in which his bani appears within the Ādi Granth displays striking linguistic and musical continuity with the surrounding Sant corpus. Its vocabulary, devotional idiom, and raga structure align closely with the bani of Ravidass and Kabir as preserved in the same recension. This coherence suggests not a later mechanical translation, but a transmission shaped within a shared spiritual and musical environment. Whether first spoken in Maharashtra or the North, the bani as received and preserved in Gurmukhi bears the imprint of an integrated devotional current — one voice among many, yet resonant in the same tonal field.

Spiritual Fellowship

The Sant tradition functioned less as a formal hierarchy and more as a fellowship grounded in Naam. Songs were carried by wandering devotees, sung in gatherings, and transmitted across regions long before written compilation stabilized them.

Namdev's Abhangs traveled northward; the bani of Ravidass resonated westward; Kabir's verses moved across linguistic boundaries. What preserved them was not centralized authorship but shared devotion.

Rather than imagining a committee of saints assembling texts, it is more historically plausible to understand that a living devotional culture safeguarded these utterances through memory, song, and mutual reverence. When later preserved in scripture, they entered written form — but their life had already endured in the hearts of devotees.

The Enduring Witness

The preserved hymns of Namdev stand as enduring testimony to a devotion that transcended region and social boundary. His voice, carried first through song and fellowship and later stabilized in sacred manuscript form, reveals a Bhakti rooted not in ritual performance but in intimate remembrance of the Divine. In one of his own lines he declares:

Chhipe ke ghar janam dailā, gur updes bhailā.

Here, worldly birth yields to spiritual awakening. The emphasis is not on origin, but on transformation through guidance and Naam. Realization is not inherited — it is awakened.

Through this principle, his light did not fade with his passing. It remained alive in the devotional current that continued to move across regions and generations — a current sustained not by hierarchy, but by remembrance.

Chapter Twenty-eight

Bhaktmal Conclusion

Bhaktmāl and the Memory of Bhakti

The Bhaktmāl tradition, initiated by Nabha Das in the late sixteenth century, represents one of the earliest systematic efforts to gather and honor the lives of the Bhakti saints of North India. Rather than composing strict historical biography, Nabha Das created a devotional register — a garland of remembered names — preserving the spiritual fragrance of those whose lives had transformed their age.

As the text circulated, later commentators such as Anantadas (c. 1588 CE) and Priyadas (1712 CE) expanded upon these brief notices. Their writings reflect deep reverence, but also the theological environments of Rajasthan and Vrindavan in which they wrote. Devotional remembrance gradually intersected with interpretation. Saints once remembered in open, experiential terms were increasingly situated within structured Vaishnava frameworks.

This development should not be read as distortion, but as theological accommodation. Later writers sought to harmonize socially transformative Sant voices with established devotional systems. In doing so, figures such as Ravidass, Kabir, Sain,

Dhanna, and Pipa were interpreted through the idiom of Vishnu-bhakti and incarnation theology.

Yet in the earliest strata of Bhaktmāl memory, certain figures appear less as disciples within inherited lineages and more as bearers of direct realization. Early portrayals of Ravidass, for example, emphasize universality — transcending caste, ritual status, and inherited rank — rather than formal sectarian placement. Later commentaries increasingly organized such open-ended figures within devotional hierarchies familiar to their own audiences.

Chronological reflection further complicates later lineage constructions. Lifespans traditionally attributed to Ramanand (variously recorded between the late 13th and early 15th centuries) overlap only partially and inconsistently with those of figures such as Ravidass (c. 1377–1527 CE), Kabir (c. 1398–1518 CE), Dhanna (b. 1415 CE), and Pipa (b. 1425 CE). When examined historically, the claim that all were direct disciples of a single teacher becomes difficult to sustain in uniform form. What emerges instead is a more fluid devotional milieu — one defined less by formal institutional succession and more by shared realization.

The preserved bani of these figures provides more reliable testimony than later narrative reconstruction. Within the Adi Granth, their voices appear not as subordinate commentary, but as integral expressions of realized devotion. These compositions speak in the immediacy of lived truth — where spiritual insight and social reality converge without reliance on ritual hierarchy or inherited authority.

The miraculous legends and symbolic visions found in later commentaries are best understood as devotional allegories. They functioned to safeguard memory, translate radical insight into

108

accessible form, and render socially transformative voices intelligible within structured religious worlds. Across such variations, a consistent principle remains: the Divine is encountered within human life itself — not confined by caste, title, or institutional boundary.

In this light, the Bhaktmāl and its commentaries reveal not merely biography, but the evolving memory of Bhakti. They show how awakened presence is remembered, interpreted, and situated across generations. Beneath these layers of interpretation remains a unifying insight: Bhakti arose not from institutional authority, but from realized experience expressed in living speech.

Bhakti as Lived by the Saints

Bhakti, as embodied by the saints, was devotion lived within the world — through honest labor, remembrance, humility, and compassion. It affirmed that the Divine is not realized through withdrawal, inherited privilege, or ritual display, but through truthful living among others. Spiritual authority arose not merely from lineage, but from awakening.

When read with discernment, the Bhaktmāl tradition does not diminish the originality of the saints; rather, it bears witness to the enduring force of their presence. Across centuries of retelling and commentary, their remembered lives continue to illuminate a vision of equality grounded in direct realization — a vision that transcends sectarian boundary while remaining rooted in lived human experience.

As Ravidass proclaims:

Jogī sar pāvahĩ nahĩ, tuā guṇ kathan apār.

Charanārbind na kathā bhāvai, supach tul samān.

Even the greatest yogis cannot reach You; Your virtues are beyond description. The teaching is clear: ascetic discipline alone cannot grasp the Infinite. True worth lies in the heart that delights in the remembrance of the Divine. Without that love, learning, status, and outward attainment carry no weight.

The path these saints chose was bhagti — not ascetic rivalry, not sectarian triumph, but shared remembrance. They walked together without discrimination of caste, creed, occupation, or gender. Their companionship did not depend upon withdrawal from society, but upon sanctifying life within it.

Within the sacred preservation of the Adi Granth, voices such as Ramananda, Namdev, Kabir, Pipa, Sadhna, Sain, and Mirabai were gathered without hierarchy. Their bani was safeguarded not by caste privilege, but by recognition of spiritual truth. The Divine was invoked under many names, yet the Voice remained one — beyond region, beyond era, beyond boundary.

That these utterances were preserved in a living script reflects more than literary effort; it reveals conscious care that sacred speech not dissolve into memory alone. Whether sung in village gatherings or inscribed upon humble leaves, the Word endured because it was lived.

The saints did not erase difference; they transcended it. In their fellowship, devotion outweighed birth, realization outweighed ritual, and love outweighed status. Bhagti, as they lived it, did not retreat from the world — it illumined it.

Chapter Twenty-nine

One Lord Many Names

God is the One Eternal Light from whom all creation flows—Infinite Consciousness, without beginning or end, nearer than breath and vaster than the sky. Known as Hari, Govind, Narayan, Ram, Allah, and Krishna, He is the compassionate Presence dwelling in every heart. Beyond all form, yet revealed through every name spoken in love, He appears where humility deepens, where the soul surrenders, and where devotion becomes the mirror of the Divine.

Tradition holds that in every age, this Light reveals a path suited to the hearts of that time. In Sat Yuga, truth was upheld through pure contemplation; in Treta Yuga, Ram embodied the way of righteousness and duty; in Dwapar Yuga, Krishna unveiled the path of divine love and wisdom; and in Kali Yuga, liberation shines through the remembrance of the Divine Name.

Across centuries and civilizations, seekers have recognized this same Light. In Bharat, it found expression in the sacred narratives of Ram and in the wisdom of the *Bhagavad Gītā* revealed through Krishna; in paths of compassion and renunciation, it was reflected through sages such as the Buddha and Mahavira; in the prophetic tradition, it was revealed as Allah through the Prophet Muhammad and preserved in the *Qur'an*; and in the West, it was proclaimed as divine mercy through Jesus and carried forward in the Gospel tradition.

In each case, the Light was not only lived but also preserved through sacred utterance—whether in epic, teaching, or revealed scripture—so that its guidance might endure beyond time. Though names, languages, and sacred histories differ, the guiding Light remains one—ever calling humanity toward compassion, truth, and remembrance of the Divine.

In the present age, this Light is most directly realized through the remembrance of the Divine Name. Within this living current of devotion, Ravidass is revered as a Thakur through whom this presence becomes manifest—not confined to ritual or lineage, but awakened in the humble heart. His utterances, preserved within the Ādi Granth, carry a depth in which a single word opens into many layers of meaning.

Thus, in the expression *"Sagal bhavan ke nāikā,"* the One is revealed as the sovereign of all realms—beyond divisions of heaven and hell—where remembrance (Naam) becomes the highest path of realization.

In this way, the voice of Ravidass emerges as both intimate and universal, guiding the seeker inward toward the same Eternal Light.

Ravidass — The Divine Name

Ravidass taught that each age carries its own spiritual foundation — truth in Sat Yuga, righteous action in Treta, and ritual worship in Dwapar — yet in Kali Yuga, liberation shines through the remembrance of the Divine Name: *"Tīno yug tīno ḍhiṛe, kal keval nām adhār."* Its expression for the age of Kali is preserved in enduring form in the Bani of Ravidass within the Ādi Granth.

Through this Bani, he offered the path of Divine Naam in a form accessible, enduring, and free from ritual or social barriers.

His Bani safeguards the seeker by declaring that without the Name of the Lord, all worldly pursuits are ultimately false: *"Har ke nām bin jhūṭhe sagal pāsāre."* Just as one calls another by name, so the Divine is remembered through Naam—simple, direct, and accessible to all. In states of realized union, Ravidass speaks in the language of non-separation:

"Tohi Mohi Mohi Tohi Antar Kaisa?"

What difference is there between You and me?

Such expressions do not elevate the individual self, but reveal the dissolving of duality in the awareness of the Divine. Ravidass does not become another God; rather, he reveals that when the veil of separation falls away, the One Light shines unobstructed.

Through Ravidass, the path for Kali Yuga stands clearly revealed — Naam, equality, and love as the true refuge.

In the language of devotion preserved in the Ādi Granth, the Divine is addressed as Thakur — a sacred name of the Lord. The Light that abides in the realized heart is the very Light that guides the world — the eternal truth that the Divine lives within every human being.

Kāhe na Vālmīkeh dekh?
Kis jāti te kih padahe amariyo, Rām bhagati bisekh?
Suān satru ajātu sabh te, Kriśan lāvai het.
Log bapurā kiā sarāhai, tīn lok praves.

Why do you not look at Valmiki?
From what caste was he, and in what station did he live — yet

through exalted devotion to Ram, he became immortal.
One whom the world considered low or unworthy — Krishna
embraced him with love.
Why should the narrow-minded world pass judgment? His
praise now resounds through all the three worlds.

In recalling Maharishi Valmiki, Ravidass reveals a deeper truth about the Divine Name. Devotion is not bound to historical sequence or physical form. Though tradition associates Ram with Treta Yuga and Krishna with Dwapar Yuga, the Reality signified by these sacred names is not limited by time. The Divine is eternal; the Name expresses that Eternal Presence.

Just as the word "Ravi" existed long before it was given to Ravidass, so the sacred names Ram and Krishna are not confined to a single earthly manifestation. They point to the Supreme Light that precedes and outlives every age. Incarnation reveals the Divine — it does not create Him.

Āpan bāpai nāhī kisī ko, bhāvan ko Har rājā.

Ravidass expresses the same truth in a simple yet profound teaching: no one belongs to anyone by birth or lineage; the Lord alone is the Sovereign of every heart. Human identity is therefore not defined by family, caste, or inherited status. All beings—women and men alike—belong to the One, and the Divine alone reigns within all. What appears divided in the world is, in truth, united in its Source.

When Ravidass uttered the names of Ram and Krishna, he invoked not a boundary but a doorway — guiding the seeker beyond form toward the One Light shining through all names. Devotion was not allegiance to many gods nor attachment to one form, but awakening to the Eternal Presence dwelling in every heart.

In this vision, Ravidass was neither bound by sect nor confined to time. He recognized the same Divine Presence in all—among sages such as Valmiki, among rulers and laborers, and within every human being. This was not speculation, but realization.

Thus, he opened the path of Naam to all—without distinction—calling each soul to remember the One, through whom all are equal and in whom all are united.

Adi Granth
Akhand Bani

Note on Usage and Reverence.

The hymns (bāṇī) referenced in this work are drawn from the Ādi Granth, where these teachings are preserved within a sacred and enduring form. The term "Ādi"—meaning primal or from the beginning—is used here with reverence for the foundational expression of the revealed Word, while acknowledging that the text is widely known today as Sri Guru Granth Sahib. Their inclusion is intended solely to illuminate and clarify the essential teachings of Ravidass, not to establish comparison, hierarchy, or evaluation among traditions. All teachings are understood within the vision of the One, all-pervading Divine Reality, present equally in every authentic path of devotion.

Before entering the Bāṇī, the reader is invited to approach it with awareness and reverence. Readers are encouraged to apply respectful honorifics—such as Sri, Guru, Satguru, Bhagat, Sant, or Sahib—according to their own tradition and devotion. The absence or variation of such titles in the text reflects considerations of consistency and readability and should not be understood as diminishing reverence.

Where possible, the Bāṇī may also be approached in its original form, through which its sound, nuance, and depth are most fully experienced.

Sarab dharam meh sresat dharam,
Har ko nām jap nirmal karam.
(Ādi Granth – p. 266)

Among all paths called religion,
the highest is this:
to remember the Name of the Lord
and to walk in purity of action.

Chapter Thirty

Dhur Ki Bani—The Word from the Primal Source

The spiritual current preserved within the Ādi Granth presents no competing voices, no divided revelations. It gathers realized utterance into a single stream. What appears as many speakers is one Light, converging in Truth.

Har so hīrā chhāḍ kai karahi ān kī āas,
Te nar dojakh jāhige, sat bhākhai Ravidass.

Kabīr bāman gurū hai jagat kā, bhagatan kā guru nāh,
Arjh urjh kai pach muā, chārau bedahu māh.

Dhūṇḍhat ḍolahi andh gat, ar chīnat nāhī sant,
Kahai Nāmā, kio pāīai bin bhagatah bhagvant.

(Ādi Granth – p. 1377; preserved in the compilation under Mehla 5)

In these utterances, the Jewel is One. The Ādi Granth does not scatter divinity into fragments; it gathers many Names into a single radiance. Like a diamond with countless facets, the One Light shines through Ram, Har, Allah, Khuda, Gosain — yet remains indivisible. To abandon this Jewel is to wander in confusion. Ritual rank, intellectual pride, inherited authority — none can polish the stone of realization. The Brahmin may master scripture, yet without devotion remains unillumined. The seeker may roam, yet without recognizing the saints, the Light is unseen. Devotion to the Divine is humility before those in whom that Light shines.

Janam maraṇ duhahū meh nāhī, jan par-upkārī āe.
Jīa dān de bhagti lāin, Har siu lain milāe.
(Ādi Granth – p. 749)

The saints are described as dwelling beyond both birth and death. Their appearance in the world is not for personal gain but for upliftment. They grant life by awakening devotion; they unite souls with the One. Their authority does not arise from position, but from realization.

Sat purakh jin jāniā, satgur tis kā nāu.
Tis kai sang sikh udhrai, Nānak har gun gāu.
(Ādi Granth – p. 286)

The True Guru is not defined by lineage, but by knowledge of the Eternal. To know the True Lord is to become the True Guide. In such company, liberation unfolds naturally. The disciple does not inherit doctrine; he absorbs Presence.

Jis ke sir ūpar tū suāmī, so dukh kaisā pāvai.
Bol na jānai māiā mad mātā, maraṇā chīt na āvai.
…
Giān dhyān kichh karam na jānā, sār na jānā terī.
Sabh te vaḍā Satguru Nānak jin kal rākhī merī.
(Ādi Granth – p. 749)

When the Lord stands as protector, fear loses its foundation. The intoxication of illusion blinds the mind, yet humility restores clarity. Wisdom, meditation, and ritual merit are insufficient without grace. Salvation in the dark age comes not through scholarship, but surrender.

Then the source is revealed:

Santahu sukh hoā sabh thāī.
Pārbrahm pūran Parmesar ravi rahiā sabhnī jāī.
Dhūr kī bāṇī āī,
Tin saglī chint miṭāī.
Dayāl purakh miharvānā,
Har Nānak sāch vakhānā.
(Ādi Granth – p. 628)

The Primal Word arises — and peace spreads everywhere. The Supreme, Perfect Lord pervades all places; nothing lies outside that Presence. This Bani is said to come from Dhur — the Eternal Source. It is not composed; it descends. It does not create division; it dispels anxiety. Compassion is its origin; Truth its expression. The saints do not manufacture revelation — they become its vessel.

And finally, the unity becomes explicit:

Koi bolai Rām Rām, koi Khudāe;
Koi sevai Gusaiyā, koi Alāh.
(Ādi Granth – p. 885)

Some utter "Ram," others "Khuda." Some serve "Gosain," others "Allah." The names vary according to tongue and tradition, yet the

Reality addressed is One. Division belongs to language; unity belongs to Truth.

Thus, within this gathered Bani, individuality does not compete — it converges. What flows through Ravidass, Kabir, Namdev, Nanak, and others is not fragmentation, but continuity. The voice is many, but the Light is one. The current is undivided; the Source is singular.

The Akhand Bani is not a collection of doctrines, but one continuous utterance flowing from the Eternal. From the Primal Word arises remembrance; from remembrance, humility; from humility, union. All arises from the One — and returns to the One.

ੴ

ੴ ਸਤਿਨਾਮੁ ਕਰਤਾਪੁਰਖੁ ਨਿਰਭਉ ਨਿਰਵੈਰੁ
ਅਕਾਲਮੂਰਤਿ ਅਜੂਨੀਸੈਭੰ ਗੁਰਪ੍ਰਸਾਦਿ ॥

Ik Oankar. Satnām. Kartā Purakh. Nirbhau. Nirvair.
Akāl Mūrat. Ajūnī. Saibhang. Gurprasād.

One Universal Creator.
Truth is the Name.
The Creative and All-pervading Being.
Without fear. Without enmity.
Timeless Form.
beyond birth. Self-existent.
Realized through the Guru's Grace.

Ik — The One

Sagal bhavan ke nāikā, Ik chhin daras dikhāe jī.

O Sovereign of all worlds, grant me Your Vision, even for one moment.

ੴ *Satgur parsad*
Har har har har har har hare.
Har simrat jan gae nistar tare.
Har ke nām Kabīr ujāgar.
Janam janam ke kāṭe kāgar.

Nimat Nāmdev dūdh piāiā.
Tau jag janam sankat nahī āiā.
Jan Ravidass Rām rang rātā.
Iu gur parsad narak nahī jātā.
(Ādi Granth – p. 487)

One Universal Reality — realized through the Grace of the
True Guru.
Har, Har, Har, Har, Har, Har, Hare.
In remembrance of the Lord, His servants cross over and are
carried to liberation.
Through the Lord's Name, Kabir shines forth;
The burdens of countless lifetimes are erased.
For Namdev, the Lord accepted even milk in loving devotion;
Thus, worldly suffering did not bind him.
Ravidass declares: dyed in the Love of the Lord,
Through the Guru's Grace, one does not fall into darkness.

Oankar—The Primal Sound

Oankar ādi mai jānā,
Likh ar meṭai tāhi na mānā.
Oaṅkār lakhai jau koī,
Soī lakh meṭaṇā na hoī.
(Ādi Granth – p. 340)

I have realized Oaṅkār as the Beginning of all.
What is inscribed by that One cannot be erased.
Whoever truly perceives Oaṅkār
knows that it is eternal and unalterable.

Preserved within the Ādi Granth, this hymn attributed to Kabir speaks not of a sectarian deity, but of Oaṅkār — the unalterable Source from which all arises.

Har — The All-Pervading One

Nāam terō āratī majan Murāre.
Har ke Nāam bin jhūṭhe sagal pāsāre.
Nāam terō āsano Nāam terō ursā, Nāam terā kesaro le chhiṭkāre.
Nāam terā ambhulā Nāam terō chandano, ghas japē Nāam le tujhai
kau chāre.
Nāam terā dīvā Nāam terō bāī, Nāam terō tel le māhi pasāre.
Nāam terē kī jot lagāī, bha-iō ujiyāro bhavan saglāre.
Nāam terō tāgā Nāam phūl mālā, bhār aṭhārah sagal jūṭhāre.
Terō kīā tujhai kiā arpau, Nāam terā tuhī chavar ḍholāre.
Das aṭhā aṭhasathe chāre khāṇī, ihai vartan hai sagal sansāre.
Kahai Ravidāss, Nāam terō āratī—
SatNām hai, Har bhog tuhāre.
(Ādi Granth – p. 694)

Ravidass declares:

The Name alone is the true ārtī. The Eternal Name is the offering itself. Here ritual is not rejected — it is interiorized. Every outer act becomes Naam. Lamp, wick, oil, garland, sandalwood — all dissolve into remembrance. The All-Pervading One is not worshiped through objects, but through awareness. Thus, the One declared as Ik becomes lived as Har — present everywhere, divided nowhere.

Satguru — The Living Lord

Sant tujhī tan sangat prāṇ,
Satgur giān jānai sant devā-dev.
(Ādi Granth – p. 486)

Satgur jāgatā hai deu.
Mālin bhūlī, jag bhulānā, ham bhulāne nāhi.
Kahu Kabīr, ham Rām rākhe, kirpā kar Har Rāi.
(Ādi Granth – p. 479)

O Saint, Your presence is my very body and breath.
The True Guru knows this wisdom —
the Saint reflects the Divine beyond all gods.

The True Guru is the Living Lord.
The world may wander in confusion, but we are not lost.
Says Kabir: the Lord has preserved me through His grace, O
Sovereign One.

Chapter Thirty-one

Satgur Mai Balihari — Ramanand

Within the Ādi Granth, the relationship between Ravidass and Ramanand is not presented through biography but through realization. The scripture does not recount outward meetings or formal lineages; instead, it preserves the moment of inner awakening — the seeker recognizing the Satguru, and the Satguru revealing the Light already dwelling within the heart.

In this vision, transmission is not a matter of institutional succession but of consciousness: an unbroken current of Nāam flowing from realization to realization. What later traditions recount through narrative and lineage, the Granth conveys through lived spiritual experience.

Thakur in the Adi Granth

Across several shabads preserved in the Ādi Granth, the word Thakur does not signify a worldly lord or the rise of an individual personality. Rather, it reveals the state in which the Divine alone is recognized as the true Master — the One acting through all.

Har āpē ṭhākur sēvak bhagat har āpē karē karāī.

The Lord Himself is Master, servant, and devotee; the Lord Himself acts and causes all to be done.

The Divine appears as Master, servant, and devotee alike — the One who offers devotion and the One who receives it.

Har āpē rav rahiā Banvārī.

The Lord Himself pervades all — Banwari dwells everywhere.

In this vision, the Thākur is not confined to a throne, a temple, or a single form. The Rav (ਰਵਿ) — the all-pervading Lord — moves through every being, revealing Himself as the giver, the receiver, and the living presence within creation.

Soleh kalā sampūran phaliā, anat kalā hoi ṭhākur chaṛiā.

All sixteen kalās blossom in fullness; beyond even these, the Thakur rises beyond limitation.

The imagery of the sixteen kalās — symbols of complete spiritual perfection — points not to human attainment but to the fullness of Divine presence manifest through realization.

Sabh nidhan das asatt sidhan ṭhākur kar tal dhariā.

All treasures and siddhis rest in the palm of the Divine.

These powers are not possessions of the individual self. They signify that every capacity, every gift, and every mystery of existence belongs to the One Reality alone.

Jo māgahi ṭhākur apune te, soī soī devai.

Whatever one asks of their own Lord, that very thing He grants.

The relationship is intimate: the seeker turns toward the Divine not as a distant ruler but as the indwelling presence sustaining all life.

Chār varan pāe pag āī.

When the four varnas bow at the feet.

The image does not celebrate social triumph; it reveals a spiritual reversal. Before realized truth, inherited hierarchies lose their authority. In the presence of awakened consciousness, distinctions of caste dissolve. Equality arises not as doctrine but as vision.

Taken together, these verses reveal a profound theological insight. The Ādi Granth does not separate the Bhagat from Thakur, nor does it reduce the Divine to a human form. Instead, the language of Bhagti dissolves the boundary entirely.

What remains is the recognition that the Lord alone acts — as Master, servant, devotee, and Doer. In this realization the voice of devotion approaches the horizon of non-duality, where all distinctions fade within the One.

What later traditions often recount through biography and lineage, the Granth preserves through realization.

Ramanand's Inner Awakening

Kat jāīai re ghar lāgo rang.
Merā chit na chalai, man bhaio pang.
Ek divas man bhaī umang.
Ghas chandan choā bahu sugandh.
Poojan chālī Brahm ṭhāe.
So Brahm batāio Gur man hī māhe.

Jahā jāīai tah jal pakhān.
Tū pūr rahio hai sabh samān.
Bed Purān sabh dekhe joi.
Ūhā tau jāīai jau īhā na hoi.
Satgur mai balihārī tor.
Jin sakal bikal bhram kāṭe mor.
Rāmānand suāmī ramat Brahm.
Gur kā shabad kāṭai koṭ karam.
(Ādi Granth – p. 1195)

Where could I go now? My home is filled with Divine color. My awareness no longer wanders; the restless mind has become still.

One day a deep longing arose within me. I ground sandalwood and prepared fragrant offerings, setting out to worship the Supreme Lord. Yet through the Guru I came to know that the very Brahm I sought outwardly dwells within the heart itself.

Wherever I look—water, stone, sky—You pervade all equally. I searched through the Vedas and the Puranas, yet why should I seek elsewhere what is already present here?

I offer myself in devotion to the Satguru, who cut away all doubt and confusion. Through the Guru's Word the burden of countless actions is erased, and Ramanand abides in the all-pervading Brahm.

The awakening described here marks a profound turning point. Ritual preparation gives way to realization. The seeker who once looked outward discovers that the Divine he sought already fills the inner being and permeates the entire world.

Ramanand's Critique of Ritualism

Tai nar kiā Purān sun kīnā.
Anapāvanī bhagat nahī upajī, bhūkhai dān na dīnā.
Kām na bisariyo, krodh na bisariyo, lobh na chhūṭiyo devā.
Par nindā mukh te nahī chhūṭī, niphāl bhaī sabh sevā.
Bāṭ pār ghar mūs birāno, peṭ bharai aprādhī.
Jih paralok jāe apkīrat, soī abidhiyā sādhī.
Hinsā tau man te nahī chhūṭī, jīa daiyā nahī pālī.
Rāmānand sādh sangat mil kathā punīt na chālī.
Chhāḍ man Har bimukhan ko sang.
(Ādi Granth p. 1253 – in some manuscript traditions attributed to
Ramanand, later classified under "Parmanand.")

What has one gained merely by listening to the Puranas?
No true devotion has arisen within, nor has the hungry been
fed.

Desire remains, anger remains, greed remains. The tongue still
clings to slander, and thus all outward service becomes empty.

One fills the stomach through wrongdoing and leaves this world
with disgrace, having practiced ignorance rather than wisdom.
Violence has not departed from the mind, nor has compassion
for living beings been nurtured.

Ramanand calls the seeker toward the company of the saints,
where sacred discourse is lived rather than merely spoken. O
mind, abandon the company of those who turn away from the
Lord.

Realization Rather Than Lineage

Later Bhaktmal traditions describe Ramanand as the guru of several northern saints, including Ravidass. The Ādi Granth, however, does not frame their relationship in biographical terms; it preserves their voices through realization rather than lineage.

Some verses historically attributed to Ramanand appear in later manuscript traditions under different names, such as Parmanand. Such shifts reflect the complex transmission of Sant poetry in early devotional communities, where realized utterances circulated widely before becoming fixed in written form.

The verses themselves portray Ramanand as a seeker transformed through inner awakening. Beginning with ritual observance and scriptural learning, he comes to recognize the Divine dwelling within the heart and pervading the entire creation. Through the Satguru's Word, doubt is cut away and the restless mind finds stillness.

The Sant Current of Kashi

In the sacred landscape of Kashi, this light of realization was not confined to a single lineage. The awakening Ramanand describes resonates deeply with the fearless declarations found in the Bani of Ravidass.

The Ādi Granth does not present a chain of authority; it reveals a shared current of realization. Where later traditions speak of discipleship, the scripture speaks of Light.

Thus the question is not who stood above whom, but where realization manifested most fully. In the presence of awakened truth, hierarchy dissolves. What remains is the recognition of the One Light shining through every illumined heart.

Ravidass appeared in humble Kashi, yet the Light of Brahm shone through him unmistakably. In that sacred city seekers encountered not lineage but realization; where the Thakur was revealed, reverence naturally followed.

The Ādi Granth itself bears witness to this spiritual reversal:

"Ab bipr pardhān tih karahi dandaut."

— Now even the highest Brahmins bow down before Me.

Whether read as poetic inversion or as social memory, the verse expresses a profound transformation. Hierarchy bends before realization. Knowledge bows before lived truth. Ritual yields before love.

In this light, the relationship between Ramanand and Ravidass need not be framed through rank or succession. Later traditions differ in their descriptions, yet the Ādi Granth preserves their voices without hierarchy — united not by institutional lineage but by realization. The awakening Ramanand describes resonates with the fearless declarations found in the Bani of Ravidass. What binds these voices is not authority, but Light.

The devotional movement they embodied required preservation. As sacred language moved from the formal world of Sanskrit into the living speech of the people, the need arose for a written form capable of faithfully safeguarding that utterance. Over time, this phonetic current took shape in what later became known as Gurmukhi — a script uniquely suited to preserve sound and transmit the Word across generations.

The variations found in early manuscripts remind us how easily names and readings could shift once living authority had passed. Such changes reveal not deliberate concealment but the fragile nature of oral and written transmission. The emergence of a stable script therefore represented more than literary development; it became a safeguard for sacred speech.

Through this preservation the Word gained a new home — not confined to temple or court, but open to all who would listen. What began as living utterance became written remembrance, ensuring that realization could endure beyond the limits of time and power.

In the sacred city of Kashi, where seekers, saints, and devotees moved within the same spiritual landscape, these voices emerged not in isolation but within a shared current of devotion. In the end, the Ādi Granth preserves not rivalry but realization. Names may shift across centuries, manuscripts may vary, and traditions may interpret them differently, yet the Light recognized by the saints remains unchanged. What Ramanand sought and what Ravidass proclaimed was not authority over another, but awakening to the One dwelling within all.

Across centuries, interpretations have differed, yet the voice preserved in the Ādi Granth remains remarkably clear. The true measure of greatness is not lineage but realization. Where the Thakur is revealed, hierarchy falls silent — and only the radiance of Truth remains.

Chapter Thirty-two

Satgur Hoe Lakhavai — Pipa

In these sacred lines preserved in the Ādi Granth, the voice of the
Sant tradition rises beyond caste and worldly power. Kingship,
ritual authority, and social rank dissolve before the realization of
the One dwelling within.

> *So brahmand pind so jān.*
> *Mān sarovar kar isnān.*
> *Sohang so jā kau hai jāp,*
> *Jā kau lipat na hoi punn aru pāp.*
> *(Ādi Granth – p. 1162)*

Know that the same Divine Presence permeates both the vast
universe and the human body. Cleanse yourself in the inner
Mansarovar — the sacred lake of the mind. Only that rare one
realizes Sohang — "I am That" who remains untouched by virtue
or vice, beyond the stain of good and evil.

> *Gur Parmesar eko jāṇ.*
> *Jo tis bhāvai so parvāṇ.*
> *(Ādi Granth – p. 864)*

Know the Guru and the Supreme Lord to be One.
Whatever pleases Him — that alone is accepted.

Gur pāras ham loh mili kanchan hoiā Rām.
(Ādi Granth – p. 1114)

Meeting the Guru—the Philosopher's Stone—I, like iron, have been transformed into gold, O Lord.

Satgur dekhiyā deekhiā leenee,
Man tan arpio antar gat keenee,
Gat mit pāee aatam cheenee.
(Ādi Granth – p. 227)

Having beheld the True Guru, the seeker receives the sacred awakening. Mind and body are offered in devotion, and the inward path is revealed. In that realization, one comes to know the true measure of the self and recognizes the Divine within.

These verses reveal a shared current of realization within the Sant tradition. The same Divine presence permeates the vast universe and the human heart; the Guru and the Supreme Lord are known as One. Kingship, caste, and learning fade before inner awakening.

The Satguru becomes the living doorway to realization, and Naam the sovereign path. In this vision, spiritual authority is not defined by lineage or rank, but by the light of realization — one Presence, one Truth.

Rājan kaun tumārai āvai?
Aiso bhāu Bidur ko dekhio, oh garīb mohi bhāvai.
Hasfī dekh bharam te bhūlā, Srī Bhagvān na jāniā,
Tumro dūdh Bidur ko pānho, amrit kar mai māniā.
Khīr samān sāg mai pāiā, gun gāvat rain bihānī,
Kabīr ko ṭhākur anand binodī, jāt na kāhū kī mānī
(Ādi Granth – p. 1105)

Satgur Parmesar merā.
Anik rāj bhog ras māṇī, nāu japī bharvāsā terā.
(Ādi Granth – p. 884)

The True Guru is my Supreme Lord.
I have enjoyed countless royal pleasures and delights, yet I
meditate on the Name, placing my trust in You alone.

This realization finds one of its clearest expressions in the hymn
of Pipa preserved in the Ādi Granth.

Kāyau devā kāyau deval kāyau jangam jāīī,
Kāyau dhūp dīp naībēdā kāyau pūjau pāīī.
Kāyā bahu khaṇḍ khojate nav nidh pāī,
Nā kachhu āibo nā kachhu jāibo Rām kī duhāī.
Jo brahmaṇḍe soī piṇḍe, jo khojai so pāvai,
Pīpā praṇavai param tat hai, Satgur ho-e lakhāvai.
(Ādi Granth – p. 695)

The body itself is the temple, and within it the living presence
of the Divine. Here are the incense, the lamp, and the sacred
offering — the worship takes place within.

Exploring this body, this universe in miniature, the seeker
discovers the nine treasures. Nothing truly comes, nothing truly
goes; all abides in the glory of the One.

The same Divine who pervades the vast cosmos dwells within
the human body. Whoever searches within shall find Him.

Says Pipa: The Supreme Essence is realized only when the True
Guru reveals it.

In this vision the outer symbols of religion are gathered into the inner sanctuary of the human heart. Temple, offering, and pilgrimage are no longer distant rites but living realization. The Divine once sought in palace and shrine is discovered within the body itself.

Such insight resonates deeply with the Sant tradition that flourished in Kashi, where seekers proclaimed that the Lord dwells not in rank, ritual, or lineage but in the awakened heart. The same current of realization flows through the fearless declarations of Ravidass and the awakening described in the verses attributed to Ramanand.

Thus the journey that began with kings and hierarchy finds its completion within the human heart. Palace, temple, and ritual fire are gathered into the body itself, where the Divine quietly abides. What Ravidass proclaimed, what Ramanand sought, and what Pipa realized converge in this truth: the Satguru reveals that the Lord is neither distant nor confined to rank, but present within all.

When this realization dawns, crowns fall away, and the soul stands sovereign in the light of Naam.

Chapter Thirty-three

Nikat Hau Tum — Mira

Within the devotional memory of North India, Mira Bai stands among the most luminous voices of Bhakti. Tradition remembers her not merely as a royal devotee of Thakur, but as a disciple of Ravidass, whom she honored as her Gurudev. In these accounts, Mira receives spiritual initiation from him and walks the path of devotion under his guidance.

Whether preserved in song, oral memory, or later manuscripts, these traditions convey a deeper truth: in the circle of saints gathered around Ravidass, spiritual authority did not belong to caste, rank, or gender. Devotion alone was the measure of the soul.

In an age when religious learning and spiritual leadership were often restricted, the presence of Mira within the Sant tradition reflects a remarkable openness. The same teacher whose words challenged caste hierarchy also welcomed seekers regardless of birth or status. Within this vision, the path of Naam belonged equally to men and women.

This understanding of the Guru is beautifully expressed in a salok preserved in the Ādi Granth under the heading Gurdev, where the Guru is described not merely as an instructor but as the very source of spiritual life and kinship.

Gurdev mātā, Gurdev pitā, Gurdev suāmī Parmesurā,
Gurdev sakhā agiān bhanjan, Gurdev bandhip sahodrā.
(Ādi Granth – p. 250)

The Divine Guru is my mother; the Divine Guru is my father;
the Divine Guru is my Lord and Supreme God.
The Divine Guru is my companion, the destroyer of ignorance;
the Divine Guru is my kinsman and brother.

In this vision the Guru stands at the center of spiritual life —
parent, companion, and guide. All who come to the Guru share
the same relationship of devotion. Before such a presence,
worldly divisions fade, and the community of seekers becomes a
single spiritual family.

It is within this atmosphere of devotion that the voice of Mira
emerges.

Kahi Ravidass, hāth pai nerai.
(Ādi Granth – p. 658)

Says Ravidass: He is nearer than our own hands and feet.

This teaching forms the foundation of Mira's devotion. If the
Divine is nearer than one's own body, then no social boundary can
separate the soul from God. The Beloved is not confined to
temple, scripture, or priesthood; He is encountered through love.

Among the devotional compositions attributed to Mira in early
manuscript traditions of the Ādi Granth appears the following
hymn in Rāg Māru. Its voice expresses the intense longing that
characterizes her devotion.

ਰਾਗੁ ਮਾਰੂ ਬਾਣੀ ਮੀਰਾ ਬਾਈ ਜੀ ਕੀ
ਮਨੁ ਹਮਾਰੋ ਬਾਂਧਿਓ ਮਾਈ ਕਵਲ ਨੈਨ ਅਪੁਨੇ ਗੁਨਾ ॥੧॥ ਰਹਾਉ ॥
ਤੀਖਣ ਤੀਰ ਬੇਧ ਸਰੀਰ ਦੂਰਿ ਗਯੋ ਮਾਈ ॥
ਲਾਗਿਓ ਤਬ ਜਾਨਿਓ ਨਹੀ ਅਬ ਨ ਸਹਿਓ ਜਾਇ ਰੀ ਮਾਈ ॥੧॥
ਤੰਤੁ ਮੰਤੁ ਅਉਖਧੁ ਕਰਉ ਤਉ ਪੀਰ ਨ ਜਾਈ ॥
ਹੈ ਕੋਊ ਉਪਕਾਰੁ ਕਰੈ ਕਠਿਨ ਦਰਦੁ ਰੀ ਮਾਈ ॥੨॥
ਨਿਕਟਿ ਹਉ ਤੁਮ ਦੂਰਿ ਨਹੀ ਬੇਗਿ ਮਿਲਹੁ ਆਈ ॥
ਮੀਰਾ ਗਿਰਧਰ ਸੁਆਮੀ ਦੈਆਲ ਤਨ ਕੀ ਤਪਤ ਬੁਝਾਈ ਰੀ ਮਾਈ ॥
ਕਵਲ ਨੈਨ ਅਪੁਨੇ ਗੁਨ ਬਾਧਿਓ ਮਾਈ ॥੩॥੧॥

Rag maru Bani Mira Bai Ji Ki
Mann hamāro bāndhiyo māī, kaval nain apune gunā. ‖ 1 ‖ *Rahāu*‖
Tīkhan tīr bedh sarīr, dūr gayo māī.
Lāgiyo tab jāniyo nahī, ab na sahiyo jāi rī māī. ‖ 1 ‖
Tant mant aaukhadh karau, ta-ū pīr na jāī.
Hai ko-ū upkār karai, kathin darad rī māī. ‖ 2 ‖
Nikat hau tum dūr nahī, beg milahu āī.
Mīrā Giridhar suāmī dayāl tan kī tapat bujhāī rī māī.
Kaval nain apune gun bādhiyo māī. ‖ 3 ‖ 1 ‖
(Ādi Granth — early manuscript and eighteenth-century traditions)

Rag maru Bani Mira Bai Ji Ki
O Mother, my mind is bound by the lotus-eyed Lord,
through His divine virtues. ‖ 1 ‖ Pause ‖
A sharp arrow has pierced my body, O Mother, When it struck,
I did not know—but now, I can bear it no longer,
O Mother. ‖ 1 ‖
I try spells, charms, and medicines, yet the pain does not leave.
Is there anyone who can help me? The agony is unbearable,
O Mother. ‖ 2 ‖
You are near to me, not far — come quickly to meet me,
O Lord. Mira's Lord, Giridhar, the Compassionate One, has
cooled the burning of her body, O Mother.

> By His lotus eyes and divine virtues, my mind is forever bound,
> O Mother. ॥3॥1॥

In this hymn the language of Bhakti becomes the language of love. The Lord's glance pierces the heart like an arrow; the pain of separation becomes the fire of devotion. No ritual or remedy can remove this wound, for it is the mark of divine attraction itself.

When Mira cries, *"You are near, not far — come quickly to meet me,"* she echoes the same realization expressed by the saints: the Beloved already dwells within. The longing of the devotee is therefore not distance, but awakening.

The fellowship of the saints is also reflected in certain headings preserved within the Ādi Granth. In some cases, a composition carries the name of one saint while acknowledging another within its transmission. Such headings hint at the shared devotional current through which Bhakti utterances were remembered, sung, and preserved across generations.

One striking example appears in Rāg Māru, where the heading reads:

Kabīr kā sabad rāg Māru, bāṇī Nāmdeo jī kī.
(Ādi Granth – p. 1105)

The Word of Kabir in Rāg Māru—the utterance of Namdev Ji.

This unusual attribution does not necessarily imply authorship in a modern literary sense. Rather, it reflects the living Sant tradition in which the voices of realized devotees often echoed and preserved one another's praise of the Divine

Kabīr kā sabad rāg Mārū, bāṇī Nāmdeo jī kī.
Chār mukat chārai sidh mil kai, dūlah Prabh kī saran pario.
Mukat bhaiō chauhūṅ jug jāniō, jas keert māthai chhatr dhario.
Rājā Rām japat ko ko na tario,
Gur updes sādh kī sangat, bhagat bhagat tā ko nām pario
Sankh chakr mālā tilak birājit, dekh pratāp jam dariō.
Nirbhau bhae Rām bal garjit, janam maran santāp hirio.
Ambrīk kau dīo abhai pad rāj, Bhabhīkhan adhik kariō.
Nau nidh ṭhākur dī sudāmai, Dhrua atal ajahū na ṭariō.
Bhagat het māriō Harnākhas, Narsingh rūp hoi deh dhariō.
Nāmā kahai bhagat bas Keshav, ajahūṅ Bali ke duār kharo.
(Ādi Granth – p. 1105)

The Word of Kabir, in Raag Maaroo — the utterance of
Namdev Ji.
The four kinds of liberation and the eight supernatural powers
gathered and took shelter at the Lord's door.
He became liberated through all the ages — divine glory
crowned his head with honor.
Who has not been saved by meditating upon Lord Ram?
By the Guru's instruction and the company of saints, he is
known among all as a true devotee.
Adorned with conch, discus, garland, and sacred tilak, such is
His splendor that even the god of death trembles.
Through the mighty strength of Ram's power, fear vanished,
and the pain of birth and death was removed.
He granted fearlessness to King Ambarik and raised Vibhishan
to greater honor.
To Sudama, the Lord bestowed the nine treasures; and Dhru
was made eternal — he has never fallen.
For the love of His devotee, the Lord slew Harnakash — taking
the form of Narasinha, the Man-Lion.

> Says Namdev: The Lord Keshav remains ever bound by His
> devotees' love, even now standing humbly at the door of King
> Bali.

The hymn itself celebrates the Lord through many sacred names:
Ram, Keshav, Narasingh, and Thakur. Each name recalls a
moment when the Divine protected a devotee — from Sudama
and Dhru to Prahlad and Bali. The message is clear: the Lord who
responds to devotion is one, though remembered through many
names and stories.

This understanding lies at the heart of the Sant tradition. The
Divine is not bound to a single name or form. The One Reality
responds to the love of the devotee.

In this sense the voices of Kabir, Namdev, and Mira do not
compete with one another; they join a single current of devotion.
Each saint speaks in a different tone, yet all point toward the same
Eternal presence.

The Living Presence: Gurudev and Thakur

The voices encountered throughout this chapter—Namdev, Kabir,
and Mira—do not stand apart. Their hymns arise from a shared
current of devotion that flowed across regions and generations
within the Sant tradition. Each praises the same Divine Reality,
remembered through many sacred names: Ram, Keshav, Giridhar,
Hari, or Thakur. The names differ, yet the Presence they invoke is
One.

At the heart of this tradition stands the Guru. In the vision
preserved in the Ādi Granth, the Guru is not merely a teacher of
doctrine but the living guide through whom the soul encounters

the Eternal. The Guru awakens the seeker to the nearness of the Divine already dwelling within.

It is in this sense that Ravidass is remembered as Gurudev. His words do not establish sect or lineage; they turn the seeker inward toward the One present in all beings. The Lord praised in devotion is the same Thakur who resides within the heart.

Thus the voices of Namdev, Kabir, Ravidass, and Mira converge in a single realization: the Divine responds not to rank or ritual, but to devotion. Before that Presence, worldly distinctions fade, and the fellowship of the saints becomes one family of seekers.

The saints call Him by many names, yet all bow before the same Thakur—the Eternal Lord who is nearer than near.

Chapter Thirty-four

Tera Arata — Dhanna

Within the fellowship of saints preserved in the Ādi Granth, the voice of Dhanna emerges as a witness to the transforming power of devotion. Remembered in tradition as a humble farmer, Dhanna represents the vision in which divine grace descends not upon rank or lineage, but upon sincerity of heart.

The path that Dhanna encountered is repeatedly described in the scripture itself as Sādh Sangat — the company of saints. In this sacred fellowship, seekers awaken to the presence of the Divine through the guidance of the Guru and the companionship of realized souls.

Sādh sangat pāī param gatē.
(Ādi Granth – p. 1293)

In the sacred company of saints, the soul attains the highest liberation.

This teaching resonates with the words of Ravidass preserved in the Ādi Granth:

Ravidass bhaṇai jo jāṇai so jāṇ,
Sant anantahi antar nāhī.
(Ādi Granth – p. 486)

Says Ravidass: only the truly wise understand this —
between the Saint and the Infinite Lord there is no difference.

In this light of spiritual equality, Dhanna stands among those
seekers who entered the current of Bhakti through the fellowship
of saints.

Sadh Sangat and Awakening

Balihārī gur apṇe, dihāṛī saad vār.
Jin māṇas te devte kīe, karat na lāgī vār.
(Ādi Granth – p. 462)

I am a sacrifice to my Guru, again and again, each day.
He transforms human beings into divine ones — and it takes
Him no time at all.

Through the grace of the Guru, illusion falls away and the vision
of the Divine is awakened. The Ādi Granth honors this sacred
fellowship where the humble are uplifted and worldly distinctions
lose their hold. Here, the measure of the soul is not birth or
status, but devotion.

Andaj jeraj setaj utbhuj, sabh varan rūp jīa jant upaīā.
Sādhū saraṇ parai so ubrai, khatrī brāhmaṇ sūd vais chaṇḍāl
chaṇḍaīā.
(Ādi Granth – p. 835)

Life arises from the egg, from the womb, from moisture, and
from the earth; the Lord has created beings of every form and
color.
Whoever seeks the refuge of the saints is saved—whether
Kshatriya, Brahmin, Shudra, Vaishya, or even a Chandala.

It is in this spirit of Sādh Sangat that figures such as Dhanna and Sain are remembered within the tradition.

Jo jo milai sādhū jan sangat, dhan Dhannā jaṭ Sain miliyā Har daīā.
(Ādi Granth – p. 835)

Whoever joins the holy company is blessed — Dhanna the farmer and Sain the barber alike encountered the Lord's compassion.

The scripture further proclaims the transforming power of this sacred fellowship:

Mahimā sādhū sang kī sunahu mere mītā.
Mail khoī koṭ agah hare, nirmal bhae chītā.
(Ādi Granth – p. 809)

Hear, O friend, the glory of the company of saints: countless impurities are washed away, and the mind becomes radiant and pure.

Here the Ādi Granth itself places Dhanna and Sain within the same sacred fellowship of seekers, affirming that the grace of the Divine descends not through birth or rank but through the refuge of Sādh Sangat.

Devotion as Service

Within the Sant tradition, the seeker who enters the company of saints becomes not a claimant of status but a servant of the Divine. The language of devotion often describes the devotee as one who has offered himself completely to the Guru and the Lord.

One such voice preserved in the Ādi Granth expresses this spirit of surrender:

Mul khareedī laalā golā, mera nāu sabhāgā,
Gur kī bachanī haat bikānā, jit lāiā tit lāgā,

...

Pīeh ta pānī ānī Mīrā, khāh ta pīsaṇ jāu,
Pakhā pherī pair malovā, japat rahā tera nāu.
(Ādi Granth – p. 991)

Here the devotee speaks as one "purchased" by love — a servant in the marketplace of grace. Wherever the Guru places him, there he remains. To fetch water, to grind grain, to fan the Lord, and to wash His feet become acts of devotion.

In this way service itself becomes remembrance. Through humility and surrender, the seeker remains absorbed in the Name of the Lord.

The Fellowship of Saints

The Ādi Granth preserves not only the individual voices of the saints but also moments in which their lives are remembered together within a single devotional vision. One remarkable hymn, placed under the heading Mahala 5, recalls several saints whose devotion transformed humble lives into spiritual realization. In this passage, figures such as Namdev, Kabir, Ravidass, Sain, and Dhanna appear within the same sacred narrative of devotion.

Gobind Gobind Gobind sang, Nāmdēu man līṇā.
Ādh dām ko chhīpro hoio lākhīṇā.
Bunnā tannā tiāg kai, prīt charan Kabīrā.
Nīch kulā jolāhrā bhaio guṇī gahīrā.

Ravidāss dhuvantā dhor nīt, tin tiāgī māiā.
Pargat hoā sādh sang, Har darsan pāiā.
Sain nāī butkārīā, oh ghar ghar suniā.
Hirde vasiā Pārbrahm, bhagtā meh ganiā.
Ih bidh sun kai jātro, uth bhagatī lāgā.
Mile pratakh Gusāīā, Dhannā vadbhāgā.
(Ādi Granth – p. 487)

In this hymn the scripture recalls how saints of humble occupations—Namdev, Kabir, Sain, and Dhanna—turned their hearts toward the remembrance of the Divine. Hearing of this path, Dhanna entered the company of saints; through devotion his life was transformed, and he came to be remembered among the bhagats.

Placed under the heading Mahala 5, the passage reflects how this fellowship of saints was preserved in the devotional memory of the tradition. Rather than separating them by status or profession, the hymn celebrates the power of devotion that united them in a single spiritual path.

Within this sacred remembrance, Dhanna appears as one who, hearing of this path, rises in devotion and encounters the grace of the Lord.

The Bāṇī further reveals the nature of such devotion:

Ghar meh thākur nadar na āvai,
gal meh pāhaṇ lai latkāvai...
Gur mil Nānak thākur jātā,
jal thal mahīal pūran bidhātā.

The Lord dwells within the home, yet one does not perceive Him;

instead, a stone is hung around the neck.
…
Meeting the Guru, says Nanak, the Lord is known—
the Perfect Creator pervades water, land, and sky.

Through the Guru's grace, the Divine is not confined to outward form but recognized as all-pervading. Read in this light, Dhanna's devotion arises within the fellowship of the sādh sangat, where the true Guru reveals the presence of the Thakur within the heart. What appears outwardly simple thus reflects an inner awakening —where faith does not remain belief alone, but matures into realization.

Dhanna's Offering of Devotion

The voice of Dhanna preserved in the Ādi Granth reflects the simplicity and depth of his devotion. His words do not present elaborate theology; instead they express the direct realization that arises through the remembrance of the Divine and the guidance of the Guru. In this hymn, Dhanna addresses the Lord as Gopāl and offers his heartfelt worship.

> *Gopāl terā āratā.*
> *Jo jan tumrī bhagat karante, tin ke kāj savārtā.*
> *(Ādi Granth – p. 695)*

O Gopal, this is my offering of worship.
Those who practice Your devotion — You Yourself complete their affairs.

> *Bhramat phirat bahu janam bilāne, tan man dhan nahī dhīre.*
> *Lālach bikh kām lubhadh rātā, man bisre prabh hīre.*
> *Bikh phal mīṭh lage man baure, chār bichār na jāniā.*

154

Gun te prīt baḍhī an bhāntī, janam maran phir tāniā.
Jugat jāni nahī ridai nivāsī, jalat jāl jam phandh pare.
Bikh phal sanch bhare man aise, param purakh prabh man bisre.
Giān praves gurah dhan dīā, dhyān mān man ek mae.
Prem bhagat mānī sukh jāniā, tripat aghāne mukt bhae.
Jot samāe samānī jā kai, achhaḷī prabh pahichāniā.
Dhannai dhan pāiā dharaṇīdhar mil jan sant samāniā.
(Ādi Granth – p. 487)

Wandering through countless births, the soul finds no peace while absorbed in greed and attachment. The mind mistakes poison for sweetness and forgets the Divine dwelling within. Yet through the Guru's gift of knowledge and meditation, the mind turns toward the One. Through loving devotion the seeker discovers true fulfillment, and the soul merges into the Divine Light.

Recognizing the Eternal Lord, Dhanna finds the true treasure and joins the fellowship of saints.

In this realization the journey described throughout the chapter finds its completion. The humble farmer who heard of the path of devotion rises through remembrance of the Divine and the company of saints. What begins in Sādh Sangat culminates in union with the Lord, where the seeker becomes one with the fellowship of saints and the presence of the Eternal.

Chapter Thirty-five

Ghar Ghar Sunia — Sain

The Fellowship of Saints

Tumre bhajan kaṭahi jam fānsā.
Bhagat het gāvai Ravidāsā.
(Ādi Granth – p. 659)

By singing Your praises, the noose of death is severed;
in the spirit of devotion, Ravidass sings.

Haj hamārī Gomti tīr.
Jahā basahī Pītambar Pīr.
Vāhu vāhu kiā khūb gāvatā hai.
Har kā nām merai man bhāvatā hai.
Nārad Sārad karahī khavāsī.
Pās baiṭhī Bībī Kavalā dāsī.
Kaṇṭhe mālā, jihvā Rām.
Sahas nām lai lai karau salām.
Kahat Kabīr Rām gun gāvau.
Hindū Turak doū samjhāvau.
(Ādi Granth – p. 478)

My pilgrimage to Mecca is on the banks of the Gomti River
where the Yellow-robed Beloved abides.
Vāhu vāhu — how beautifully He sings!

The Name of the Lord delights my heart.
Narad and Sarada stand in attendance;
beside Him sits Kamala, the devoted handmaiden.
A rosary at the neck, "Rām" upon the tongue,
I bow again and again, uttering the thousand Names.
Says Kabir: singing the praises of the Lord,
both Hindu and Turk are instructed alike.

Kabir speaks not of a figure bound to time, but of the Eternal Presence revealed in song—where all names and forms are known as One. Within this same sacred current, remembrance continues, and another voice rises in that living stream of devotion.

Sain is remembered in the Ādi Granth not through lineage or status, but through devotion and service. His name appears in verses that preserve both his longing for the Divine and the grace through which he was liberated.

Āvahu sajṇā hau dekhā darsan terā Rām.
Ghar āpṇṛai kharī takā mai man chāu ghanerā Rām.
(Ādi Granth – p. 764)

Come, O Beloved, that I may behold Your Vision, O Lord.
Standing within my own home, I wait and watch—my heart
filled with deep longing for You, O Lord.

Within the home itself, longing awakens—waiting, watching, filled with yearning.

Āu jī tū āu hamārai, har jas sravan sunāvanā.
Tudh āvat merā man tan hariā, har jas tum sang gāvanā.
Sant kirpā te hirdai vāsai, dūjā bhāu miṭāvanā.
(Ādi Granth – p. 1018)

158

Come, O Beloved, come into my presence, that I may hear the
Lord's praise.
At Your arrival, my mind and body blossom; with You I sing
the Divine Glory.
By the grace of the saints, He dwells within the heart, and
duality is erased.

These lines express longing fulfilled through fellowship. Devotion
ripens through the fellowship of saints.

Satgur kī sevā safal hai, je ko kare chit lāi.
Man chindiā phal pāvaṇā, haumai vichahu jāi.
Bandhan toṛai, mukat hoi, sache rahai samāi.
Is jag meh nām alabh hai, gurmukh vasai man āi.
Nānak jo gur sevahi āpṇā, hau tin balihārai jāu.
(Ādi Granth — p. 644)

The service of the True Guru is fruitful when performed with
focused awareness. Ego dissolves, bonds are broken, and one
remains absorbed in the Eternal.

Though not composed by Sain, these lines articulate the spiritual
condition his life reflects — selfless service, freedom from ego,
and the Name dwelling within.

Nāī udhariyo Sain sev.
(Ādi Granth — p. 1192)

The barber Sain was liberated through service.

The verse magnifies not occupation, but devotion expressed
through service. Through humble service performed without
pride, Sain crossed beyond limitation.

Har kī vaḍiāī dekhahu santahu,
Har nimāṇiā māṇ devāe.
Jiu dharatī charan tale te ūpar āvai,
tiu Nānak sādh janā jagat āṇ sabh pairī pāe.
(Ādi Granth – p. 735)

Behold the greatness of the Lord, O Saints—
the Lord bestows honor upon the humble.
As the earth, though beneath the feet, remains above, so, says
Nanak, the world comes and falls at the feet of the holy.

Sain naai butkārīā oh ghar ghar suniā.
Hirde vasiā Pārbrahm bhagtā mahī ganiā.
(Ādi Granth – p. 487)

Sain the barber became heard in every household.
The Supreme dwelt within his heart, and he was counted among
the devotees.

"Ghar ghar suniā" suggests more than reputation — it signifies
remembrance. Devotion echoed through homes because the
Divine had found dwelling in his heart.

The nature of this devotion is further illuminated in the Bāṇī:

Bhagautī Bhagavant bhagat kā rang.
(Ādi Granth – p. 274)

The Divine Power is the very color of devotion to the Lord.

Bhagautī here is not an external force, but the living current of
devotion through which the Lord is known.

In the Divine Voice of the Ādi Granth, a Bhagat is not merely a
devotee by outward practice, but one in whom the Divine

presence abides. Such a person is counted among the realized, beyond distinctions of caste, profession, or worldly rank. In this sense, Sain stands among those whose hearts became the dwelling place of the Supreme, and through whose remembrance the Divine Name spread from home to home.

His remembrance stands within a wider fellowship of saints.

Namdev Kabīr Trilochan Sadhna Sain tarai,
(Ādi Granth – p. 1106)

Namdev, Kabir, Trilochan, Sadhnā, and Sain are recalled together — not by caste, trade, or region, but by realization. The scripture gathers saints across time into one current of devotion.

In this testimony preserved in the Ādi Granth, Ravidass speaks with quiet certainty of those who crossed the ocean of existence through devotion. Their names appear together as witnesses that spiritual realization belongs not to status or birth, but to remembrance of the Divine—voices walking the same path of devotion.

Within this sacred fellowship, devotion becomes a living current that awakens hearts across regions and communities.

Dhoop deep ghrit saaj aartee,
Vaarane jaau kamlaa patee.
Mangalaa har mangalaa,
Nit mangal raajaa raam raay ko.
Ootam dee-araa nirmal baatee,
Tuheen niranjan kamlaa paatee.
Raamaa bhagat Raamaanand jaanai,
Puran paramaanand bakhaanai.
Madan moorat bhai taar Gobinde,

Sain bhanai bhaj paramanande.
(Ādi Granth – p. 695)

Incense, lamps, and pure ghee are prepared for the divine Aarti
I offer myself in reverence to the Lord of Lakshmi, the Beloved
of the Lotus.
Auspicious, ever auspicious is the Lord;
Eternal are the blessings of King Ram, the Sovereign of all.
The lamp is pure, its flame stainless and bright;
You alone are the Spotless One, Lord of the Lotus.
Whoever is a devotee of Ram is known as a Ramanandu;
He speaks of the Supreme Bliss as perfect and complete.
The beautiful Divine Form removes the fear of the world, O
Gobind!
Says Sain — meditate upon the Supreme Bliss!

In this hymn, Aarti is no longer ritual alone — it becomes interior
offering. The incense, the lamp, and the flame symbolize the
awakened heart. The true light is not external; it is the presence of
the Divine within.

Sain does not magnify ceremony; he transforms it. Worship
becomes self-surrender, and the soul itself becomes the lamp
placed before the Eternal.

His words stand in harmony with the broader current preserved in
the Ādi Granth, where devotion transforms ritual into
remembrance and the heart into a dwelling of the Divine.

Though the Bhagats preserved in the scripture lived in different
regions and centuries, their voices converge in a single current of
longing and realization. In that convergence, distinctions fade and
devotion becomes the common language.

Sain's Aarti is therefore not spectacle but surrender. Through love and humility the heart becomes radiant, and where the Name dwells, ordinary life is illumined.

Chapter Thirty-six

Mai Nahi — Sadhna

Kahai Kabīr sunahu re santahu, khet hī karahu nibērā.
Ab kī bār bakhas bande kau, bahur na bhaujāl pherā.
(Ādi Granth – p. 1104)

Says Kabir: listen, O Saints—settle the account here in this very
field.
Grant forgiveness to this servant now, that there may be no
return to the ocean of existence again.

Within the language of the Sant tradition, such cries for release
appear across many voices of the saints. The saints repeatedly
describe the human condition as standing within the bhaujāl—the
vast ocean of existence—from which only divine grace can deliver
the soul.

One such utterance preserved in the Ādi Granth proclaims:

Mai nāhī kachh āh, na morā,
Tan dhan sabh ras Gobind torā.
(Ādi Granth – p. 336)

Nothing remains as mine; I claim nothing as my own.
My body, my riches, and all delight are Yours, O Gobind.

This utterance echoes the very tone that defines Sant prayer — complete surrender, absence of ownership, and the offering of self to the Divine. Such resonances across the Adi Granth reveal a shared spiritual vocabulary among the saints. Whether voiced by one or another, the language of egolessness binds them together.

Sadhnā, remembered in the Ādi Granth through both his own supplication and in the sacred enumeration alongside Namdev, Kabir, Trilochan, and Sain, stands within this living fellowship of saints.

> *Namdev Kabīr Trilochan Sadhna Sain tarai,*
> *(Ādi Granth – p. 1106)*

The verse affirms that liberation is not confined to lineage or geography. Saints of different regions, centuries, and social backgrounds are remembered together — united not by birth, but by realization.

> *Nrip kanniā ke kāranai ik bha¬iā bhekhdhārī.*
> *Kāmārthī suārthī vā kī paij savārī.*
> *Tav gun kahā jagat gurā jao karam na nāsai.*
> *Singh saran kat jāīai jao jambuk grāsai.*
> *Ek būnd jal kārāne chātrik dukh pāvai.*
> *Prān gaye sāgar milai funi kām na āvai.*
> *Prān jo thāke thir nahī kaise birmāvau.*
> *Būd mūe naukā milai kaho kāhi chaḍhāvau.*
> *Mai nāhī kachh ha¬o nahī kichh āh na morā.*
> *Ausar lajjā rākh leho Sadhnā jan torā.*
> *(Ādi Granth – p. 858)*

For the sake of a king's daughter, one man became a renunciate. But he did it only for desire and selfish gain — yet You, O

Lord, still preserved his honor.

O Guru of the world, how can Your virtues be described, when even one's karma cannot be erased?

Where could the deer find refuge, if the jackal were to devour the lion?

For just one drop of water, the rainbird (chatrik) suffers in agony.

If life departs, even the vast ocean can no longer be of any use.

When the breath itself is tired and failing, how can anyone be reassured?

If one drowns and dies, what good is a boat found afterward?

I am nothing, I have nothing— nothing belongs to me.

At this moment, please preserve my honor, for Sadhna is Your servant.

The declaration *"mai nāhī… na morā"* expresses the deepest insight of Sant devotion: the disappearance of "I" and "mine." When the sense of ownership dissolves, the soul stands entirely before the Divine, sustained only by grace.

In this hymn, Sadhnā speaks not as a philosopher but as one standing at the edge of helplessness. The imagery is urgent: a drowning man, a fading breath, a rainbird longing for a single drop. Each metaphor intensifies the same truth — human strength cannot rescue itself.

The refrain *"lajjā rākh leho"* — preserve my honor — reveals the heart of Sant devotion. It is not pride that seeks protection, but surrender. The devotee entrusts his dignity entirely to divine grace.

Tradition places Sadhnā in Sindh in the twelfth century, yet in the Ādi Granth his voice stands beside saints from many regions and eras. Not as chronology, but as continuity. The scripture preserves not eras, but realization.

Sadhnā does not argue caste. He does not assert status. He asks only for grace. And in that humility, he joins the fellowship of saints remembered together — where devotion surpasses lineage, and surrender transcends social rank.

Through this hymn, the Sant path becomes unmistakable: when all supports fail, only remembrance remains. And in that remembrance, the soul is carried across.

Chapter Thirty-seven

Santan Sang — Kabir

Within the fellowship of the Sant tradition, Kabir stands as one of the most luminous voices preserved in the Ādi Granth. His Bani speaks not of sect or lineage, but of the universal Light that shines equally in all beings.

Universal Light

Aval Allah nūr upāiā, kudrat ke sabh bande.
Ek nūr te sabh jag upjiā, kaun bhale ko mande.
(Ādi Granth – p. 1349)

In the beginning, the One Divine Light was brought forth; from that Light came all beings of creation.
From the One Light the entire world arose — so who can be called good, and who can be called bad?

In this proclamation preserved in the Ādi Granth, Kabir addresses humanity at its deepest root. Before caste, before creed, before temple or mosque — there is Light. All emerge from a single Source.

Within this vision, superiority and inferiority lose their meaning. No one stands above another; no one is condemned by birth. The question "who is good, who is bad?" becomes a challenge to every constructed division. Unity precedes judgment.

Santan sang Kabīrā bigariyo,
So Kabīr Rāmai hoi nibariyo.
(Ādi Granth – p. 1158)

In the fellowship of the Saints, Kabir was transformed;
In that divine company, Kabir was absorbed in the Lord.

The word bigariyo does not imply corruption, but undoing — the breaking of ego, the loosening of self-identity. In the presence of realized beings, Kabir describes a spiritual re-formation.

What dissolves is not the body, but the illusion of separateness. What remains is remembrance.

The Bani here speaks not of legend, but of inner transformation — of ego melting into Divine awareness. The path is not mythic elevation, but spiritual refinement.

Yak arj guftam pes to dar gos kun Kartār,
Hakā Kabīr Karīm tū beaib Parvardigār.
(Ādi Granth – p. 721)

I place one humble petition before You — listen, O Creator:
You alone are the True One — the Great, the Compassionate, the Flawless Sustainer.

In this passage preserved in the Ādi Granth, the voice turns to Persian devotional vocabulary — Karīm, Parvardigār, Kartār. These were living sacred expressions of the 15th-century spiritual world.

The word Kabīr here resonates within the vocabulary of Islamic devotion. In Arabic, al-Kabīr signifies "The Great," one of the Divine attributes. The supplication therefore directs attention entirely toward the greatness of the Creator.

The fellowship between saints is also reflected in the Bani itself. Within the Ādi Granth, Ravidass refers to Kabir directly, recognizing the radiance born through the remembrance of the Divine Name.

Har ke nām Kabīr ujāgar,
Janam janam ke kāṭe kāgar.
(Ādi Granth – p. 487)

Through the Lord's Name, Kabir shines radiant and pure;
the karmic records of countless lifetimes have been erased.

Here Ravidass affirms the transforming power of Naam as manifest in Kabir. Kabir is described as ujāgar — illumined, revealed, made radiant through Divine remembrance. The radiance belongs not to the individual but to the transforming power of the Lord's Name.

Jā kai Īd Bakrīd kul gāū re badh karahi, mānīahi sheikh shahīd pīrā,
Jā kai bāp vaisī karī, poot aisī sarī, tihū re lok prasidh Kabīrā.
(Ādi Granth – p. 1293)

Ravidass acknowledges the inherited religious customs of Kabir's lineage — shaped by Islamic observance and reverence for sheikhs and pīrs. As the father practiced, so did the sons follow.

Yet the verse moves immediately to transformation: Kabir became renowned throughout the three worlds. His renown did not arise from inherited identity, but from realized truth. Divine grace, not ancestry, became the measure of stature.

> *Dārid dekh sabh ko hasai, aisī dasā hamārī.*
> *Asat dasā sidh kar talai, sabh kirpā tumārī.*
> *(Ādi Granth – p. 858)*

Seeing the outward, worldly state, people mock—such is the condition.
Yet the eight supernatural powers and the ten mystical perfections lie beneath the hand, all through Your grace.

The world judges by appearance; grace works unseen. What seems lowly outwardly may conceal spiritual abundance. All is attributed not to the self, but to Divine compassion.

In Ravidass's Bani, this current flows as one stream of grace. Kabir is not praised for birth, nor for social standing, but for illumination through Naam. Lineage is acknowledged, yet it does not confine destiny.

Transformation, not inheritance, defines renown.

Kabir, Namdev, Trilochan, Sadhna, or Sain — each stands as testimony that Divine remembrance dissolves the weight of karma and the boundaries of caste.

The radiance is one, the Source is one, and the grace that carries the saints across the ocean of existence is one.

The Voice of Kabir — Devotion to the Satguru

> *Satguru mile ta mārag dikhāiā,*
> *Jagat pitā merai man bhāiā.*

Kahu Kabīr jan eko būjhiā,
Gur parsād mai sabh kichh sūjhiā.
(Ādi Granth – p. 476)

When I met the True Guru, He revealed the path to me;
and the Lord, Father of the world, became pleasing to my heart.
Says Kabir: this servant has realized the One;
by the Guru's Grace, everything has become clear.

Kabir begins not with self-assertion, but with gratitude. The path was shown; it was not self-discovered. The turning of the heart toward the Divine followed the meeting with the Satguru. Through the Guru's grace, the One became known, and the confusion of the world fell away.

Satigur kīno par-upkār,
Kāḍh līn sāgar sansār.
(Ādi Granth – p. 331)

The True Guru has shown the highest kindness;
He lifted me from the ocean of worldly existence.

Here the metaphor is unmistakable: without the Guru, one drowns; through the Guru, one is carried across. Liberation is described not as achievement, but as rescue.

Kabīr sāchā Satgur mai miliā,
sabad ju bāhiā ek.
(Ādi Granth – p. 1372)

Kabir says: I have met the True Satguru,
who struck me with the One Shabad.

The Shabad is not mere instruction — it is awakening. The "blow" is the moment of awakening. The ego is pierced; remembrance becomes steady.

In the preserved Bani, Kabir speaks repeatedly of the Satguru as revealer, rescuer, and awakener. The path was revealed; the ocean was crossed; the Word struck the heart.

Transformation did not arise from self-effort alone, but through the grace of the Satguru.

Kabir does not glorify himself. He attributes everything to the Guru — guidance, protection, awakening, and liberation. Yet Kabir's awakening unfolds not only through the Satguru, but also through the living fellowship of saints. The language is intimate, reverent, and deeply relational.

What emerges is not a figure claiming authority, but a disciple formed through the compassion of the Satguru.

Kabir and the Shelter of the Saints

Hamro bhartā baḍo bibekī, āpe sant kahāvai.
Oh hamārai māthai kāim, aur hamrai nikaṭ na āvai.
(Ādi Granth – p. 476)

My Beloved is supremely wise; He Himself is called the Saint.
He stands firm above my head in protection; no other comes near me.

Here the Saint and the Lord are not divided. Divine Wisdom manifests as protective presence. This protection is not worldly power, but spiritual steadiness.

174

Hau māṅgau santan renā.
Mai nāhī kisī kā denā.
(Ādi Granth – p. 656)

I ask only for the dust of the Saints' feet;
I owe nothing to anyone.

Kabir does not seek status or authority. His longing is for the dust of the Saints — the lowest place, yet the safest.

Kabīr jam kā ṭheṅgā burā hai, oh nahī sahiā jāi,
Ek ju sādhū mohi miliyo, tinh līā añchal lāi.
(Ādi Granth – p. 1368)

Kabir says: the blow of Death's staff is terrible— no one can endure it.
But when a Saint met me, he gathered me lovingly into the fold of his protection.

Here the Saint becomes shelter. Fear yields to refuge. The image of being gathered into the hem of the garment expresses intimacy and protection.

Pūrab janam ham tumhre sevak, ab tau miṭiā na jāī,
Tere duārai dhun sahaj kī, māthai mere dagāī.
(Ādi Granth – p. 970)

From previous births I have been Your servant; this bond shall never be erased.
At Your door resounds the melody of natural peace, and upon my forehead You have placed the mark of grace.

The relationship is not temporary. It is ancient and enduring. The "mark" signifies belonging — not ritual identity, but spiritual imprint.

Rām mo kau tār kahāṅ lai jaī hai,
(Ādi Granth – p. 1104)

Lord, where could You take me now to rescue me?

The question itself expresses trust. Having found shelter, there is nowhere else to turn.

In these hymns preserved in the Ādi Granth, Kabir speaks not as an isolated mystic, but as one sheltered in holy company. The Saint protects from the fear of death; the Satguru rescues from the ocean; the Divine Beloved stands guard.

Kabir does not portray himself as self-made or self-sufficient. His awakening unfolds within grace — through the Guru, through the Shabad, through the fellowship of the Saints.

Delusion of the Ego — Baure

Within the Divine Bani, spiritual delusion is often described as a kind of madness—the mind intoxicated by pride, status, and self-importance.

Ham baḍ kab kulīn, ham paṇḍit, ham jogī sannyāsī.
Giānī gunī sūr ham dāte, ih budh kabahū na nāsī.
Kahu Ravidass sabhai nahee samajhas, bhool pare jaise baure"
(Ādi Granth – p. 974)

I am a great poet, of noble lineage; I am a Pandit, a yogi, a renunciate.
I am wise, virtuous, brave, and generous— such self-conceit

176

never fades.
Few understand this truth; people wander in delusion like the mad.

Ravidass here exposes the illusion created by ego. Titles, learning, and reputation easily become instruments of pride, and the mind becomes intoxicated by its own self-importance. Those trapped in such thinking move through the world like the bewildered, unable to perceive the Divine within.

Kabir describes the same state using the language of divine "madness," where worldly cleverness dissolves and only the remembrance of the Lord remains.

Bidiā na parau, bād nahī̃ jānau.
Har gun kathat sunat baurāno.
Merē bābā, maĩ baurā—sabh khalak saiāṇī, maĩ baurā.
Maĩ bigriō, bigrai mat aurā.
Āp na baurā, Rām kīō baurā.
Satgur jār ga-iō bharam morā.
Maĩ bigrē apnī mat kho-ī.
Merē bharam bhūlau, mat koī.
So baurā jo āp na pachhānai.
Āp pachhānai, ta ēkai jānai.
Abahi na mātā, su kabahu na mātā.
Kahi Kabīr, Rāmai rang rātā.
(Ādi Granth – p. 855)

I do not pursue formal learning, nor do I engage in debate; speaking and hearing the virtues of the Lord, I am called mad.
O my father, I am mad— the whole world is clever; I alone am mad.

Kabir explains that true madness lies not in devotion but in forgetting the self's divine origin. One who fails to recognize the inner self wanders in confusion, but one who truly knows the self recognizes only the One. Thus Kabir declares that he is "mad" only because he is dyed in the love of the Lord.

In the language of the saints, this "madness" is the undoing of ego. What the world calls madness is, in truth, awakening—when pride dissolves and the heart becomes absorbed in the remembrance of the Divine.

True and False Saints

Gaj sāḍhe tai tai dhoñā, tihre pāin tag.
Galī jinhā japmālīā, loṭe hath nibag.
Oi Har ke sant na ākhīahī, Bānāras ke ṭhug.
Aise sant na mo kau bhāvahī.
Ḍālā siō peḍā gaṭkāvahī.
Bāsan māñj charāvahī ūpar, kāṭhī dhoī jalāvahī.
Basudhā khod karahī dui chūlhē, sāre māṇas khāvahī.
Oi pāpī sadā phirahī aparādhī, mukhahu aparas kahāvahī.
Sadā sadā phirahī abhimānī, sagal kuṭamb ḍubāvahī.
Jit ko lāiā tit hī lāgā, taise karam kamāvai.
Kahu Kabīr, jis Satgur bheṭai, punarap janam na āvai.
(Ādi Granth – p. 476)

They wear heavy cloaks and spotless loincloths, sacred threads hang around their necks.
Rosaries dangle at their throats, water-pots rest in their hands.
But these are not to be called saints of the Lord; they are deceivers of Benares.

Kabir warns that outward signs of holiness can easily conceal pride and hypocrisy. Robes, threads, rosaries, and ritual display cannot reveal the truth of the heart. A person may appear pious while remaining bound by greed and ego, sustaining divisions of status, caste, or identity. Such figures wander proudly in the world while misleading others with the appearance of sanctity.

For Kabir, the mark of the true saint is not costume or reputation but awakening through the Satguru. Only the one who meets the True Guru is freed from the cycle of birth and death.

> *Ravidāss bhaṇai jo jāṇai so jāṇ.*
> *Sant anantahi antar nāhī.*
> *(Ādi Granth – p. 486)*

Ravidass says: whoever understands, understands.
Between the Saint and the Infinite there is no separation.

In this simple declaration, Ravidass expresses the essence of sainthood. The saint is not distinguished by outward signs, but by union with the Infinite. Where such realization arises, there is no distance between the human and the Divine.

Kabir's Own Voice on Birth and Identity

In many later devotional traditions, saints are surrounded by stories that attempt to elevate or reshape their origins. Yet Kabir's own Bani preserved in the Ādi Granth speaks with remarkable clarity about his social background and spiritual path. Rather than concealing his birth, Kabir openly acknowledges it — while simultaneously dissolving its importance through devotion to the Divine.

Jāt julāhā mat kā dhīr,
Sahaj sahaj guṇ ramai Kabīr.
(Ādi Granth – p. 328)

Born in the caste of weavers, yet steady in wisdom,
Kabir weaves the virtues of the Lord with effortless grace.

Tū̃ bāmhan, mai Kāsīk julhā, būjhahu mor giānā,
Tumh tau jāche bhūpat rāje, Har sau mor dhiyānā.
(Ādi Granth – p. 482)

You may be a Brahmin, and I but a weaver of Kashi — yet
grasp the knowledge
I share: you look to earthly kings for your support, but my heart
remains absorbed in the Lord alone.

Māthe tilak, hath mālā bānā.
Logan Rām khilaunā jānā.
(Ādi Granth – p. 1158)

With the sacred mark on the forehead and the rosary in hand,
they make a show of devotion—
people treat the Lord's Name, Ram, as nothing more than a toy.

Kabīr prīt ik siu kīe, ān dubidhā jāi,
Bhāvai lāmbe kes karu, bhāvai gharar muḍāi.
(Ādi Granth – p. 1365)

Kabir says: Make your love devoted to the One alone — and let
all other doubts fall away.
Whether you keep long hair or shave your head completely,
none of these outer forms matter.

Gagan damāmā bājio, pario nīsānai ghāu,
Khet ju māṇḍio sūramā, ab jūjhan ko dāu.
Sūrā so pahichānīai, ju larai dīn ke het,
Purjā purjā kaṭ marai, kabhū na chhāḍai khet.
(Ādi Granth – p. 1105)

The drum resounds in the sky; the battle standard is struck.
The field has been set by the brave—now is the time to fight.
Only that one is known as a warrior who fights for righteousness.
Even if cut limb by limb, he dies standing firm and never abandons the battlefield.

Kabir's own Bani therefore leaves little ambiguity about how he understood himself. He acknowledges his birth among the Julāhās of Kashi without hesitation, yet immediately dissolves the significance of caste through devotion to the Divine. In Kabir's vision, the measure of a person is not lineage, ritual marks, or religious costume, but remembrance of the One. The saint's authority arises not from inherited status, but from realization of truth.

Kabir on Birth and the Illusion of Sacred Geography

In later devotional literature, the lives of saints are sometimes surrounded by miraculous narratives intended to emphasize their spiritual greatness. Yet Kabir's own Bani preserved in the Ādi Granth speaks in a strikingly direct and human voice. Rather than presenting himself as a figure born outside the natural order, Kabir repeatedly speaks of life within the ordinary conditions shared by all humanity.

Jaise māt pitā bin bāl na hoī,
Bimb binā kaise kapre dhoī.
Ghor binā kaise asvār,
Sādhū bin nāhī darvār

.....

Kahai Kabīr ekai kar karnā,
Gurmukh hoi bahur nahī marnā.
(Ādi Granth – p. 872)

Just as no child can be born without mother and father,
as no cloth can be cleansed without water,
as no rider can travel without a horse,
so without the Saint, there is no royal court of the Lord.
...
Kabir declares: do only one thing with your whole being—
 become a Gurmukh, and you shall never suffer death again.

Kabir uses simple images drawn from everyday life: a child cannot exist without parents, cloth cannot be cleaned without water, and a rider cannot travel without a horse. Through these comparisons he emphasizes a universal truth: spiritual awakening, like life itself, unfolds within the natural order of creation.

Kāshī Maghar sam bīchārī.
Ochhī bhagat kaise utaras pāri.
(Ādi Granth – p. 326)

Consider Kashi and Maghar to be the same— with shallow devotion,
How will one ever cross to the other shore?

Kabir also dismisses the belief that salvation depends upon dying in a particular place. For him, Kashi and Maghar are the same;

without sincere devotion, no location can carry the soul across the ocean of existence.

Kabir's own words therefore point consistently toward simplicity and truth. Birth follows the natural order of life, and liberation does not depend upon geography or outward circumstance. What matters is devotion to the One and the guidance of the Satguru. In Kabir's vision, the path to freedom lies not in miraculous origins or sacred locations, but in the transformation of the heart.

> *Kabīr merā mujh mahi kichh nahī, jo kichh hai so terā.*
> *Terā tujh kau saupate, kiā lāgai merā.*
> *(Ādi Granth – p. 1375)*

Nothing within me is mine; whatever exists belongs to You.
What is already Yours I return to You—what then can be called mine?

In this final confession Kabir expresses the heart of devotion. When the illusion of ownership dissolves, the soul recognizes that everything belongs to the Divine. In that surrender the seeker finds freedom, and the One Light shines without division.

Within the hymns of the saints preserved in the Ādi Granth, sacred speech began to move from living utterance into written preservation. The wisdom of Kabir, Namdev, Ravidass, and many others was gathered into a single sacred treasury so that the voice of realization might endure beyond the lifetimes of the saints themselves.

Through this preservation the Sant fellowship continues to speak across generations. Kabir's vision of the One Light, shining equally in all beings, remains alive wherever the Divine Name is remembered and the illusion of separation falls away.

Chapter Thirty-eight

Tu Mero Thakur — Namdev

Within the sacred verses preserved in the Ādi Granth appears a remarkable declaration linking the vision of Namdev with the later appearance of Ravidass:

Ūch te ūch Nāmdeo samdarsī,
Ravidāss ṭhākur baṇ āī.
(Ādi Granth – p. 1207, Mehla 5)

Exalted among the exalted is Namdev, the seer of equality;
Ravidass has appeared as the Divine Lord — the Thakur of all.

The verse joins two great voices of the Sant tradition within a single line. Yet historically these saints did not belong to the same generation. Namdev is generally placed in the late thirteenth and early fourteenth centuries, while Ravidass appeared decades afterward.

The statement therefore does not describe a physical meeting between the two saints. Instead, it reflects a deeper continuity within the devotional current that flowed across generations. Namdev is remembered as a samdarsī—one who perceives the Divine equally within all beings. In that same spiritual current, the appearance of Ravidass is described as the manifestation of the Divine Thakur.

Seen in this light, the verse preserved in the Ādi Granth becomes a recognition of spiritual realization rather than a chronological record. The vision of equality embodied by Namdev finds its fullest expression in the presence of Ravidass.

To understand the depth of this recognition, one must listen carefully to the hymns of Namdev preserved within the Ādi Granth. Within these hymns the voice of devotion becomes so intimate that the boundary between the devotee and the Divine often disappears.

The Divine Voice in the Bani of Namdev

Merī bāndhī bhagat chhaḍāvai,
bāndhai bhagat na chhūṭai mohi.
(Ādi Granth – p. 1252)

My devotee may free others from My bonds,
yet I cannot free Myself from the bond of My devotee.

In this striking declaration, the Divine voice reverses ordinary power. God is no longer distant and untouchable; instead, the Lord becomes bound by the love of the devotee. Such expressions reveal the extraordinary intimacy that defines the Sant path.

Another verse reflects the mysterious destiny of Namdev's birth:

Chhipe ke ghar janam dailā,
gur updes bhailā.
(Ādi Granth – p. 486)

By the Guru's command I took birth in the house of a Chhipa;
through the Guru's teaching, realization awakened.

Here the birth of the saint is not described as an accident of caste but as a deliberate unfolding of divine purpose.

Elsewhere the unity between the devotee and the Divine becomes even more direct:

Nāme Narayan nāhī bhed.
(Ādi Granth – p. 1166)

Between Namdev and the Lord Narayan there is no separation.

This line expresses the culmination of devotional realization: the devotee and the Divine are no longer experienced as separate.

Namdev's bani repeatedly moves beyond outward religious divisions. In one celebrated verse, he observes the differing practices of communities yet points beyond them both:

Hindū pūjai dehurā, musalmāṇ masīt,
Nāme so-ī seviā, jah dehurā na masīt.
(Ādi Granth – p. 875)

The Hindu worships in the temple, the Muslim in the mosque; but Namdev serves the One who dwells beyond both temple and mosque.

In another hymn preserved within the Granth, the dialogue becomes almost playful in its intimacy:

Tū kun re?
Mai jī, Nāmā.
(Ādi Granth – p. 694)

"Who are you?"
"It is I… Nāmā."

Such moments reveal a relationship in which the devotee stands before the Divine without distance or fear.

Ravidass also proclaims the incomparable stature of the true devotee:

Pandit sūr chhatrapat rājā —
bhagat barābar aur na koe.
(Ādi Granth – p. 858)

Scholar, warrior, emperor, and king—
none stand equal to the devotee.

The Ādi Granth even preserves a beloved narrative hymn in which the Lord Himself accepts the offering of His devotee:

Ek bhagat mere hirdai basai,
Nāme dekh Narāin hasai.
Dūdh pīāi bhagat ghar gaiā,
Nāme Har kā darshan bhaiā.
(Ādi Granth – p. 1163)

"One devotee dwells within My heart," says the Lord.
Seeing Namdev's love, Narayan smiles.
The Lord drinks the milk offered in devotion,
and Namdev returns home blessed with the vision of the Divine.

So complete is this relationship that the Divine voice finally declares:

Kahah ta dharan ikorī karao,
Kahah ta le kar ūpar dharao.
(Ādi Granth – p. 1166)

If you command, I will tilt the earth to one side;
if you wish, I shall turn it completely upside down.

Here devotion reaches its highest expression: the Lord Himself responding to the love of the devotee.

Recognition of Namdev Among the Saints

The reverence shown toward Namdev is not limited to later tradition; it appears directly within the sacred verses preserved in the Adi Granth. Other saintly voices acknowledge the depth of realization found in his devotion.

In one hymn attributed to Kabir, both Jayadev and Namdev are remembered as exemplars of divine love:

Gur parsādī Jaideu Nāmāṅ,
Bhagati kai prem in hī hai jānāṅ.
(Ādi Granth – p. 330)

By the Guru's grace, Jai Dev and Namdev attained realization,
for they knew that true devotion lies in divine love.

Here devotion is defined not by ritual or status but by prem—the living love through which the soul unites with the Divine.

Rejection by Society, Acceptance by the Divine

Despite this spiritual recognition, Namdev's path was not free from worldly scorn. In another hymn preserved in the Granth, society is described as mocking him because of his birth:

Nāmdēu prīt lagī Har setī,
lok chhīpā kahai bulāe.
Khatri Brāhmaṇ piṭh de chhode,

Har Nāmdēu īā mukh lāe.
(Ādi Granth – p. 733)

Namdev's heart was bound in love with the Lord, yet people
mocked him and called him a "Chhippā."
The proud Kshatriyas and Brahmins turned away from him, but
the Lord embraced Namdev and raised him to honor.

In this verse the Sant tradition reverses the social order. Those
rejected by society are lifted by the Divine, while pride and
hierarchy are left behind.

The Path of the Guru

The Sant path repeatedly emphasizes that such realization is not
attained through birth or learning but through the grace of the
Guru:

Gur bin sahaj na ūpjai,
bhāī pūchhahu giānīā jāi.
Satgur kī sevā sadā kar,
bhāī vichahu āp gavāi.
(Ādi Granth – p. 638)

Without the Guru, the natural state does not arise—ask the
wise and they will tell you.
Serve the True Guru always, O brother, and erase ego from
within.

Through this teaching the path becomes clear: humility, service,
and the dissolving of the self within the wisdom of the Satguru.

Tu Mero Thakur

The culmination of Namdev's devotion appears in a hymn where the relationship between the devotee and the Divine unfolds as a sacred play:

Badahu kī na hoḍ Mādhav mo siu.
Thākur te jan, jan te Thākur, khel pari¬o hai to siu.

...

Kahat Nāmdeu, tū mero ṭhākur, jan ūrā tū pūrā.
(Ādi Granth – p. 1252)

Why not enter into this divine play with me, O Mādhav?
From Lord to servant and from servant to Lord—
such is the sacred game between us.

...

Says Namdev: You are my Thakur;
I am empty, and You alone are complete.

In these lines the devotee does not seek elevation or status. The highest realization appears as surrender—the servant emptying himself so that the Divine alone may remain.

Marathi Echoes in the Sacred Bani

Among the hymns preserved in the Adi Granth, certain verses attributed to Ravidass display linguistic forms that closely resemble the devotional idiom of western India. These expressions echo the language associated with the poetry of Namdev, whose hymns emerged within the Marathi-speaking bhakti world.

Though separated by region and generation, the voices of these saints resonate through a shared spiritual language.

Ravidass and the Language of the Saints

One such hymn of Ravidass proclaims the sanctity of the company of saints:

> *Sant tujhī tan sangat prān,*
> *Satigur giān jānai sant devā dev.*
> *Sant che sangat sant kathā ras,*
> *Sant prem mājhāi dījai devā dev.*
> *Sant ācharan sant cho mārag,*
> *sant cho olhag olhagnī.*
> *Aur ik māgau bhagat chintāmaṇi,*
> *Jaṇī lakhāvahu asant pāpī saṇ.*
> *Ravidāss bhaṇai jo jāṇai so jāṇ,*
> *Sant anantahi antar nāhī.*
> *(Ādi Granth – p. 486)*

O Saint, You are my very body, my sacred company, and my
life-breath.
The True Guru knows divine wisdom — the Saint is the very
God of gods.
The company of the Saints is the sweetest of nectars;
Grant me a place in the love of Saints, O Lord of all Lords.
The path of the Saints is pure, their conduct holy;
they walk in divine humility, step by step, with grace.
I ask for only one gift — the jewel of devotion;
and may I clearly discern the false and sinful from the true.
Says Ravidass: he alone is truly wise who knows this —
that between the Saint and the Infinite Lord, there is no
difference.

This hymn repeatedly celebrates the sangat of saints, describing their company as the nectar of divine love and affirming that the realized saint and the Infinite Lord are not separate.

Namdev and the Marathi Devotional Tradition

A hymn of Namdev preserved in the Granth expresses a similar realization through another metaphor:

> *Ād jugād jugād jugo jug, tā kā ant na jāniā,*
> *Sarab nirantar Rām rahiā, Ravi aīsā rūp bakhāniā.*
> *Gobid gājai, sabad bājai,*
> *Ānand rūpī mero Rāmaīā.*
> *Bāvan bīkhū bānai bīkhe, bās te sukh lāgilā,*
> *Sarbe ād paramlād kāṣṭ chandan bhaiilā.*
> *Tumh che pārash, ham che lohā, saṅge kanchan bhaiilā,*
> *Tū daiyāl ratan lāl, Nāmā sāc samāilā.*
> *(Ādi Granth – p. 1351)*

From the beginning of time, through all the ages and beyond, none have ever found His limits.
The Lord pervades all; He shines everywhere — like the radiant sun whose light fills all space.
The Lord resounds as the music of creation, and within that divine melody my soul rejoices — for my Lord is the very form of bliss.
Even from the poison of the world arises fragrance;
by His touch, pain turns to sweetness.
By His presence, even dry wood becomes sandalwood — the lowly is made precious through His grace.
You are the touchstone, O Lord, and I am mere iron — by union with You, I am transformed into gold.

> You are merciful, the jewel beyond price; says Namdev — I am absorbed in Your Eternal Truth.

Here Namdev describes the Divine as a touchstone that transforms iron into gold. Through contact with the Divine, the ordinary is transfigured into the radiant.

A Shared Spiritual Language

Placed side by side, these hymns reveal a deep spiritual harmony between the voices of Ravidass and Namdev. Ravidass speaks of the sweetness of the saints' company — *"sant chī sangat sant kathā ras"* — while Namdev describes the transforming grace of the Divine touch — *"tumh che pārash, ham che lohā."*

Such echoes suggest that the devotional language associated with Namdev's tradition continued to resonate within the wider Sant movement. The appearance of similar linguistic forms in the bani of Ravidass hints at the wide circulation of these devotional expressions across regions and generations.

Together, their hymns proclaim the same realization: in the presence of the Divine, the humble is transformed, and the saint and the Infinite are recognized as one light.

The Milk Offering of Namdev

Within the hymns preserved in the Adi Granth, a beloved devotional episode appears in which the Lord accepts milk offered by Namdev.

The memory of this event is first hinted at in a verse attributed to Ravidass, where the saint recalls Namdev's offering:

Nimat Nāmdēu dūdh pīāiā,
Tau jag janam saṅkaṭ nahī āiā.
(Ādi Granth – p. 487)

Through Namdev's humble devotion, the Lord Himself drank
the milk offered by his hand;
thereafter the burdens of worldly suffering no longer troubled
him.

The episode appears in fuller poetic form within a hymn of
Namdev preserved in the Granth:

Dūdh kaṭorai gaḍvai pānī,
Kapal gāi Nāme duhi ānī.
Dūdh pīu Gobinde rāi,
Dūdh pīu mero man patīāi.
Nāhī ta ghar ko bāp risāi.
Soin kaṭorī amrit bharī,
Lai Nāme Har āgai dharī.
Ek bhagat mere hirdai basai,
Nāme dekh Narāin hasai.
Dūdh pīāi bhagat ghar gaiā,
Nāme Har kā darshan bhaiā.
(Ādi Granth – p. 1163)

The bowl is filled with milk, the vessel with water;
Namdev milks the sacred cow and brings the offering before
the Lord.
"O Lord Govinda, drink this milk," he prays,
"for my heart will find peace when You accept it.
If You refuse, even my father will be displeased."
Namdev fills a golden bowl and places it humbly before the
Divine.

Seeing the devotion of His servant, Narayan smiles.
"One devotee dwells within My heart," the Lord declares.
Accepting the offering, the Lord drinks the milk from
Namdev's hand.
Thus the devotee returns home blessed,
having received the vision of the Divine.

The Temple Turns Toward the Devotee

Ahankārīā nindakā piṭh dei, Nāmdēu mukh lāiā.
(Ādi Granth – p. 451)

The Lord turned His back on the arrogant and the slanderers,
and turned His face toward Namdev.

Hast khelat tere dehure āiā,
Bhagat karat Nāmā pakar uṭhāiā.
Hīnaṛī jāt merī, jādim rāiā,
Chhīpe ke janam kāhe kau āiā.
Lai kamlī chaliyo palṭāi,
Dehurai pāchhai baiṭhā jāi.
Jiu jiu Nāmā Har guṇ ucharai,
Bhagat janāṅ kau dehurā phirai.
(Ādi Granth – p. 1164)

Namdev came to the temple in simple devotion. As he bowed
before the Lord, the priests seized him and drove him away.
They questioned his birth in the family of a Chhīpā.
Wrapping himself in his blanket, Namdev went behind the
temple and sat there in quiet devotion.
Yet as he continued to sing the praises of the Lord, a wonder
occurred: the temple itself turned to face the devotee.

In this hymn the message of the Sant tradition becomes unmistakable. When pride and social distinction rejected the devotee, the Lord Himself rejected that pride. The temple that had excluded Namdev turned instead toward the one whose heart was filled with devotion.

Thus the hymn affirms a truth echoed throughout the Bani: the Divine does not dwell where pride rules, but where love and humility abide.

The Voice of Devotion

The milk-offering episode preserved in these hymns carries the intimate tone of a dialogue between the Lord and His beloved devotee. The imagery of the golden bowl, the smiling Lord, and the Divine acceptance of the offering expresses a relationship that transcends ritual form.

In this sacred moment the milk becomes the symbol of the devotee's heart. The Lord's acceptance reveals the central truth of the Sant path: the Divine does not remain distant but responds to the love of the devotee.

From the brief remembrance preserved in the verse of Ravidass to the fuller narration found in the hymn of Namdev, the message remains the same: where devotion is pure, the Lord Himself becomes present.

The Voices of the Sants

Within the sacred hymns preserved in the Adi Granth, the saints often appear not as isolated voices but as a fellowship of realization. One verse of Ravidass recalls several of these figures together:

Nāmdēv Kabīr Tilōchan Sadhnā Sain tarai,
Kahai Ravidāss sunahu re santahu, Har jīu te sabhai sarai.
(Ādi Granth – p. 1106)

Namdev, Kabir, Tilochan, Sadhna, and Sain have crossed the
ocean of existence.
Says Ravidass: listen, O Saints—through the grace of the Living
Lord, all are carried across.

In this remembrance the saints are not distinguished by birth or
region, but are united in devotion to the One.

Among these saints, the voice of Namdev speaks with the
humility of one who knows his complete reliance upon the
Divine.

Mo kau tār le Rāmā, tār le,
Mai ajān jan taribe na jānau, bāp Bīṭhulā bāh de.
Nar te sur hoi jāt nimakh mai, Satigur budh sikhlāī,
Nar te upaj surag kau jītio, so avakhadh mai pāī.
Jahā jahā dhūa Nāradu ṭeke, naik ṭikāvahu mohi,
Tere nām avilamb bahut jan udhare, Nāme kī nij mat eh.
(Ādi Granth – p. 873)

"O Lord, carry me across," he prays. "I am ignorant and do not
know the path. O Father Vitthal, extend Your hand and save
me." Through the wisdom of the True Guru, the ordinary
human becomes radiant with divine understanding. By the
power of the Divine Name, countless souls are liberated—this
is Namdev's own realization.

The same insight appears in the hymns of both Namdev and Pipa, who affirm that the highest truth is revealed through the True Guru:

Māi na hotī, bāp na hotā, karam na hotī kāiā.
Ham nahī hotē, tum nahī hotē, kavan kahān te āiā?
  ...
Nāmā praṇavai param tat hai, satgur ho-e lakhāiā.
(Ādi Granth – p. 973)

If there were no mother, no father, no body formed through karma, then neither you nor I would exist—who then could say from where we came?
...
Says Namā: the Supreme Essence is known only when the True Guru reveals it.

Pīpā praṇavai param tat hai, Satgur ho-e lakhāvai.
(Ādi Granth – p. 695)

Says Pipa: the Supreme Essence is realized only when the True Guru reveals it.

The path to this realization is repeatedly described as the company of the saints:

Sādhsangat pāī param gate.
(Ādi Granth – p. 1293)

Through the fellowship of the saints, the soul attains the highest state.

And as Trilochan teaches:

Anti kāl Nārāin simrai,
aisī chintā mahi je marai,
Badat Trilochan, te nar muktā,
pītambar vā ke ridai basai.
(Ādi Granth – p. 526)

One who remembers the Lord at the final moment
and leaves this world absorbed in such remembrance—
says Trilochan—that soul is liberated,
for the Lord Himself dwells within their heart.

In these hymns the voices of the saints converge into a single realization. Whether it is Namdev calling upon Vitthal, Pipa proclaiming the revelation of the Guru, or Trilochan remembering the Divine at life's final breath, each voice speaks the same truth: the path to liberation lies in devotion, humility, and the remembrance of the One.

Thus the Sant fellowship preserved in the Adi Granth stands as a living testimony that the grace which carried Namdev across the ocean of existence continues to guide every seeker. In that current of realization, Namdev is remembered as the seer of equality, and in that same light the presence of Ravidass shines forth—fulfilling the sacred line:

"Ūch te ūch Nāmdeo samdarsī,
Ravidāss ṭhākur baṇ āī."

The Merchant of the Divine Name

Within the hymns of the Divine voice, the image of the banjāra—the traveling trader who carries and spreads the wealth of the Divine Name — appears as a symbol of the soul traveling through the world while bearing the true treasure of remembrance.

In one such hymn, Ravidass speaks in this voice:

Ko banjāro Rām ko,
merā ṭāṇḍā lādiyā jāe re.
Hau banjāro Rām ko,
sahaj karau vāpaār.

Maĩ banjāran Rām kī,
Terā Nāam vakhar vāpaār jī.

Ardas — The Prayer of the One

Tū ṭhākur, tum pahi ardās.
Jīu piṇḍ sabh terī rās.
Tum māt pitā, ham bārik terē.
Tumrī kirpā mahi sūkh ghanē rē.
Koi na jānai tumrā ant.
Ūchē te ūchā bhagvant.
Sagal samagrī tumrai sūtar dhārī.
Tum te hoi so āgiākārī.
Tumrī gat mit tum hī jānī.
Nānak dās sadā kurbānī.
(Ādi Granth – p. 268)

You are the Thakur — to You alone is my prayer.
Body and breath are held in Your trust.
You are Mother and Father; we are Your children.
Within Your grace dwell countless comforts.
No one knows Your limit.
Highest of the high, O Divine Sovereign.
All creation is strung upon Your thread;
whatever arises moves by Your command.
Your mystery and measure are known only to You.
Says Nanak: Your servant is forever devoted.

Origins and Evolution
of Gurmukhi Script

੯. Punjabi Literary Traditions

In the study of linguistic and literary history, it is important to distinguish between a language and the script used to record it. Punjabi refers to the spoken and literary language of the Punjab region, while Gurmukhi, Shahmukhi, and Devanagari are writing systems that have been used by different communities to represent that language. The existence of Punjabi speech or poetry in earlier centuries does not necessarily imply the presence of a particular script at the same time, since many traditions circulated orally long before they were written down.

Some historical narratives associate the emergence of Punjabi literary expression with earlier yogic or devotional communities. Yet from the perspective of manuscript evidence and historical linguistics, the precise relationship between those traditions and the development of the Gurmukhi script remains a matter of scholarly discussion. To date, no extensive surviving textual corpus from those communities has been clearly identified in that script.

When examining the historical record, it is likewise difficult to identify large numbers of early Punjabi manuscripts written in Gurmukhi. Many scholars therefore note that some of the earliest preserved examples of Punjabi devotional expression appear within later compilations that gathered sacred hymns and spiritual teachings, including verses attributed to earlier saints such as Baba Farid and Bhagat Sadhna.

By the sixteenth century, Punjabi poetic activity expanded with figures such as Shah Hussain, Bhai Gurdas, and Pilu. Among these, the writings of Bhai Gurdas hold particular importance. His Vars survive in early manuscripts written in the Gurmukhi script and represent one of the earliest substantial bodies of Punjabi literary expression preserved in that writing system.

In the seventeenth century Punjabi literature continued to flourish through poets such as Sultan Bahu, Baba Bulleh Shah (Meri bukkal de vich chor), and Ali Haider Multani, whose works were often recorded in the Shahmukhi script, reflecting the Persian-influenced literary culture of the time.

The eighteenth century witnessed the development of the Punjabi qissa tradition, with poets such as Hashim Shah and Shah Mohammad composing narrative works that blended folklore, romance, and social reflection. Among the most celebrated of these works is Heer-Ranjha by Waris Shah, a composition that vividly reflects the cultural life and imagination of Punjabi society.

During the nineteenth century, literary scholarship expanded through figures such as Pandit Tara Singh Narotam, Shradha Ram Phillauri, Dhani Ram Chatrik (Punjab karan ki sift teri), and Sahib Singh, among others who contributed to the study and development of Punjabi literature.

The twentieth century saw the emergence of modern Punjabi literature with writers such as Bhai Vir Singh, Amrita Pritam, Mohan Singh, Kulwant Singh Virk, Balwant Gargi, Surjit Patar, Shiv Kumar Batalvi, Sant Ram Udasi, Charan Singh Safri and Dalip Kaur Tiwana, among other notable figures.. Through their works, Punjabi literature continued to flourish in both Gurmukhi and Shahmukhi scripts, extending the reach of the language and connecting new generations to its rich literary heritage.

Gurmukhi Lipi Da Janam Te Vikas

The antiquity of the Gurmukhi script is increasingly supported by historical evidence. Multiple independent sources indicate that a script closely resembling early Gurmukhi was in active use in Punjab well before its later standardization during the Guru-period.

S. G. B. Singh, in his study of the origin and development of Gurmukhi, presents traced facsimiles and reproductions of stone inscriptions found on the walls of Rai Firoz's mausoleum in the village of Hathur (District Ludhiana, Punjab). These inscriptions are dated to 1470, 1497, 1497, 1501, and 1516 CE (corresponding to Vikram Samvat 1527, 1554, 1554, 1558, and 1573). Their presence on a public monument demonstrates that this script was not experimental or private, but already established and legible within the region.

These inscriptions, dated in Vikram Samvat as ੧੫੨੭, ੧੫੫੪, ੧੫੫੪, ੧੫੫੮, and ੧੫੭੩, are carved on the walls of Rai Firoz's mausoleum and correspond to the late fifteenth and early sixteenth centuries, confirming the active use of Gurmukhi during that period.

Earlier evidence associated with the same site was reported by Sur Atar Singh Bhadauriya (1833–1899 CE), who informed Dr. G. W. Leitner of a damaged stone inscription dated to 1419 CE. Bhadauriya later referenced another inscription from 1476 CE in an article presented to the Royal Asiatic Society. Although these earlier inscriptions have suffered erosion over time, their recorded existence further strengthens the case for a pre-Guru Gurmukhi tradition.

Additional confirmation comes from a different sphere. On 31 July 1916, Lala Shivdayal, M.A., writing in The Tribune, noted that the genealogical registers (vahis) maintained by pandas of Kangra, Gaya, and Hardwar contain specimens of a script resembling Gurmukhi that predate the Sikh Gurus. As continuously maintained ritual records, these vahis provide valuable evidence of everyday script usage beyond formal literary contexts.

Taken as a whole, inscriptional evidence, scholarly documentation, and archival records support the conclusion that Gurmukhi existed as a living script in Punjab prior to its later formalization. Its significance lies not only in its antiquity but in its transformation: through its use in preserving revealed bani, it became a medium shaped by sound, rhythm, and spoken expression rather than by classical grammatical systems alone. In this sense, Gurmukhi functioned not as a structure imposed upon speech, but as one aligned with it.

This understanding accords with the traditional expression "from the mouth of the Guru"—not as a claim of invention, but as a recognition that the authority of the script arises from lived and spoken transmission within an earlier Satguru-centered devotional environment. In this role, Gurmukhi becomes more than a writing system: it serves as a medium through which utterance is carried across generations, preserving continuity between voice and form.

Punjab

As noted in Gurmukhi Lipi Dā Janam te Vikās, the designation Punjab is of relatively late usage. It appears in Mughal administrative records during the reign of Emperor Akbar around 1590 CE, and only later came to be widely associated with the expression "Land of Five Rivers"—the Sutlej, Beas, Ravi, Chenab, and Jhelum.

Prior to this period, the region did not exist as a single unified political entity. Instead, it comprised multiple cultural and agrarian zones identified through local communities and patterns of settlement. Within such a fluid landscape, linguistic and devotional traditions moved freely across boundaries, unconfined by later administrative definitions.

This context helps explain how a phonetic script such as Gurmukhi could circulate organically through speech, devotion, and everyday practice before the consolidation of regional identity.

Gurmukhi Lipi Da Itihas

As discussed in Gurmukhi Lipi Dā Itihās, the Akharī Bānīs composed by the Sikh Gurus reflect a process of documentation and stabilization rather than the creation of an entirely new script. In Guru Nanak's Paṭṭī, the ordering of letters begins with Sassā (ਸ), while in Oankar the sequence appears as "ੳ ਸ ਪ ੜ ੲ", indicating an already recognizable structural form. This arrangement continues in Guru Amar Das's Paṭṭī and is preserved in Guru Arjan Dev's Bāvan Akharī as "ੳ ਸ ਪ ੜ."

These compositions record the script as it functioned in lived usage, emphasizing letter order, phonetic clarity, and structural consistency rather than identifying a point of origin. In doing so, they provide stability and canonical form to a writing system already in circulation.

As further noted by Piyara Singh Padam, several writing systems were active across northern India during this period, including Śāradā in Kashmir, Ṭākrī in the western hills, and Laṇḍā scripts among merchant communities of Punjab and Sindh. The presence of shared letter forms—approximately twenty to twenty-five characters—suggests a broader environment of script development rather than direct derivation. Within this context, Gurmukhi emerges as a distinct and refined script shaped for phonetic clarity and functional precision.

Gurmukhi as a Linguistic and Social Medium

Modern linguistic scholarship further supports the functional strength of the Gurmukhi script. As noted in Punjabi Bhassa Dā Vikās by Duni Chand, the development of language and script is closely linked with social progress, as systems of sound and writing evolve alongside changes in awareness, education, and social organization.

Punjabi followed this trajectory, developing into multiple regional dialects—Majhi, Malwai, Doabi, Puadhi, Bagri, Pothohari, Shahpuri, Jangli–Rangri, Hindko, Saraiki, and Jatki—many of which have long employed Gurmukhi and Shahmukhi as primary scripts. The suitability of Gurmukhi lies in its phonetic structure: its thirty-five letters effectively represent the range of Punjabi sounds with clarity and consistency.

In this light, Gurmukhi functioned not only as a medium for devotional and literary expression but also as a reflection of broader cultural and social development. Its endurance reflects a script grounded in speech, capable of preserving language, memory, and meaning across generations.

੨. The Early Spread of Gurmukhi

During the late fourteenth and fifteenth centuries, northern India witnessed the emergence of several influential devotional voices, including Ravidass (c. 1377–1527 CE), and Kabir (c. 1398–1518 CE). Their teachings circulated widely through oral instruction, devotional song, and itinerant gatherings. In this environment, spiritual realization was not transmitted through fixed institutions but through the living exchange of speech, remembrance, and shared devotion.

Within the Divine Voice preserved in the Ādi Granth, realization is repeatedly presented as the awakening brought by the Divine Word itself rather than the result of ascetic disciplines or yogic systems. The hymns remind the seeker that the Infinite cannot be grasped through bodily techniques or speculative knowledge. As one verse proclaims:

Jogī sar pāvahĩ nahĩ, tuā guṇ kathan apār.
(Ādi Granth – p. 346)

Even the greatest yogis cannot reach You; Your virtues are beyond all description.

The Bani further declares:

Thit vār nā jogī jāṇai, rut māhu nā koī.
Jā kartā srishṭī kau sāje, āpe jāṇai soī.
(Ādi Granth – p. 4)

No yogi knows the exact moment or the day; no one knows the
season or the month.
The One who created the universe — only He Himself knows.

In this light, the preservation of sacred utterance emerges not
from yogic institutions but from the realized voices whose hymns
were gathered in the Ādi Granth. These compositions therefore
represent one of the earliest extensive bodies of devotional
speech preserved in the Gurmukhi script, bearing witness to a
tradition in which the Divine Voice itself becomes the source of
written expression.

The emergence of early Gurmukhi aligns closely with the
fifteenth and early sixteenth centuries, a period marked by
widespread itinerant teaching and oral transmission. Figures
described in the Bani as *"sant anantahi antar nāhī"* (ਸੰਤ ਅਨੰਤਹਿ ਅੰਤਰੁ ਨਾਹੀ
— "there is no difference between the saint and the Infinite")
traveled across regions, carrying their teachings through spoken
instruction, devotional song, and shared practice rather than
through centralized institutions.

Historical references indicate that saints traveled along settlement
routes, trade paths, and pilgrimage centers, allowing teachings and
linguistic practices to circulate organically across regions. In such a
setting, a script shaped primarily by sound rather than by classical
grammatical systems would naturally accompany oral
transmission, serving the needs of preservation rather than
institutional control.

Within this environment, the need for a clear and practical phonetic script arose to preserve teachings transmitted through voice. While the script itself developed through historical processes, the devotional milieu in which these teachings were shared played a central role in shaping its use and continuity.

Archaeological evidence supports the presence of such a script during this period. Early Gurmukhi inscriptions at the Tomb of Rai Firoz (1470–1516 CE) demonstrate that a recognizable form of the script was already in use in Punjab during the late fifteenth century, coinciding with a time of active devotional teaching where literacy and spiritual instruction intersected.

The networks through which these teachings spread extended across social boundaries. Figures such as Raja Pipa, along with Sain and Dhanna, are remembered within the sant tradition, illustrating how devotional language and script moved fluidly between communities—from royal households to everyday life.

Alphabetic devotional compositions from this era suggest the presence of an established phonetic framework. Works such as *Bāvan Akharī* reflect familiarity with structured letter sequences integrated into devotional expression.

Taken as a whole, chronological context, inscriptional evidence, itinerant teaching networks, and alphabetic compositions—the early spread of Gurmukhi is best understood as the result of lived transmission rather than sudden institutional creation.

Shared Devotion and Transmission

If the script came to be known as Gurmukhi—"from the mouth of the Guru"—the term may reflect a tradition in which knowledge was transmitted orally through recognized spiritual authority. Rather than implying invention in written form, it points to the teaching of sound, pronunciation, and meaning through which the full range of letters was understood and preserved.

Further insight appears in the Vārs of Bhai Gurdas, which describe saints gathering at the homes of fellow devotees for extended periods of collective kirtan, often referred to as Rainsubāī kīrtan. These accounts portray a devotional culture grounded in presence, repetition, and shared memory rather than formal institutional structures.

Within this environment, alphabetic awareness functioned not merely as literacy but as reflection. In Kabir's Bāvan Akharī, preserved in the Ādi Granth, the structured use of letters reflects an established phonetic system already active within devotional practice.

Manuscript traditions beyond Punjab, including those associated with the Dadu Dayal Panth, preserve the bani of Ravidass in Gurmukhi form. Their presence across regions indicates that the script traveled alongside the teachings themselves, while their phonetic consistency reflects participation in a shared linguistic environment shaped primarily by oral authority.

Collectively, devotional gatherings, alphabetic compositions, manuscript circulation, and enduring tradition support the view that Gurmukhi matured within a Satguru-centered environment of living transmission. Its refinement emerged gradually through shared practice and preserved utterance rather than through later institutional design.

3. Gurmukhi — The Written Voice of the Divine Bani

Within the Divine Bani preserved in the Ādi Granth, references repeatedly appear to letters, writing, and the recording of sacred utterance. These reflections point toward an important moment in the history of devotion: the living voice of realization beginning to take written form so that its wisdom might be preserved and shared across generations.

One striking image appears in the Bani of Ravidass:

> *Tar tār apavitr kar mānīai re, jaise kāgrā kart bīchārṁ.*
> *Bhagat bhāgaut likhīai tih ūpare pūjīai kar namaskārṁ.*
> *(Ādi Granth – p. 1293)*

The palmyra palm tree is considered impure, and its leaves are regarded as impure as well.
But when the words of devotion are written upon a page made from those very leaves, people bow in reverence and offer worship before it.

Through this image, Ravidass reminds us that sanctity does not lie in the material object itself. The palm leaf remains the same—but when the Divine remembrance is written upon it, the page becomes worthy of honor. What transforms the ordinary into the sacred is the presence of the Divine Word.

Ravidass likewise reflects on the relationship between sacred knowledge and written letters:

Nānā khiyān purān bed bidh chauntīs akhar mānhī.
(Ādi Granth – p. 658)

The many Shastras, the Puranas, and the Vedas are all composed within the thirty-four letters.

In this brief line, Ravidass reminds us that the great bodies of sacred learning are expressed through ordered letters. Written language therefore becomes a vessel through which knowledge is preserved and transmitted across generations.

Kabir speaks of this transmission in another profound passage:

Divas rain tere pāu palosau, kes chavar kar ferī. …
Gur dīnī bastu Kabīr kau, levahu bast samhār.…
Kabīr dīī sansār kau, līnī jis mastak bhāg.
Amrit ras jin pāiā, thir tā kā sohāg.
(Ādi Granth – p. 969-970)

Day and night I wash Your sacred feet, O Lord; with my hair I wave the chaur in reverence.…
The Guru has given Kabir a precious treasure, saying: "Receive this gift and guard it carefully."…
Kabir offers this treasure to the world; yet only that one receives it upon whose forehead such destiny is written.
One who tastes the immortal nectar of this gift — his union with the Divine becomes everlasting.

Within these lines Kabir speaks not of personal possession but of transmission. What he received from the Guru is described as a treasure, entrusted to him and offered to the world. The gift does

216

not belong to one community or one generation; it is presented openly to all who are able to receive it.

In this way the Bani itself portrays sacred teaching as a living inheritance — received from the Guru, preserved through remembrance, and shared with humanity.

Within the Bani, the word sikh appears in its original sense as a learner or disciple—one who receives the teaching of the Satguru. Kabir reminds the seeker that the presence of the Guru alone is not sufficient; the disciple must also be receptive to the teaching:

Kabīr sāchā Satgur kiā karai, jau sikhā meh chūk.
Andhe ek na lāgaī, jiu bāns bajāīai phūk.
(Ādi Granth – p. 1372)

Kabir says: what can the True Guru do if the disciple is at fault? Nothing reaches the blind — like blowing into a hollow bamboo flute without sound.

Here Kabir uses the word sikhā in its most fundamental sense: the seeker who learns from the Satguru. In this early devotional language, a sikh is defined not by identity but by the discipline of learning and inner transformation. The teaching may be spoken, yet its meaning is realized only when the heart is open to receive it.

Yet Kabir also reminds us that letters themselves are not the final truth:

Bāvan achhar lok trai sabh kachh in hī māhi.
E akhar khir jāhige, oi akhar in mah nāhi.
(Ādi Granth – p. 340)

Through these fifty-two letters the three worlds and everything within them are described.
Yet these letters shall fade away; the Imperishable One cannot be contained within them.

The saints therefore acknowledge both realities at once. Letters are necessary for preserving wisdom, yet the Divine Reality itself transcends written symbols. The script becomes a vessel, but the essence remains the living Shabad.

Kabir expresses the intimacy of this realization in another celebrated line:

Kabīr man nirmal bhaeā jaisā Gangā nīr.
Pāchhai lāgo Har phirai kahat Kabīr Kabīr.
(Ādi Granth – p. 1367)

Kabir says: my mind has become pure like the waters of the Ganga.
Now the Lord Himself walks behind me, calling out "Kabir, Kabir."

This image reveals the heart of the Sant path: when the mind becomes pure through remembrance of the Divine Name, the distance between seeker and the Divine disappears.

Within this tradition the Shabad itself becomes the Guru:

Bāṇī Gurū, Gurū hai Bāṇī, vich Bāṇī amrit sāre.
Gur Bāṇī kahai sevak jan mānai, paratakh Gurū nistāre.
(Ādi Granth – p. 982)

The Word is the Guru, and the Guru is the Word; within the Word lies the essence of the nectar.

When the Guru speaks the Word and the servant accepts it, the manifest Guru delivers him.

Here the authority of the teaching lies not in lineage, institution, or social identity, but in the Bani itself. The Word becomes the guide for every seeker who approaches it with humility.

At the same time, the Bani cautions that speech lacking the guidance of realized truth remains incomplete:

Satgurū binā hor kachī hai Bāṇī.
Bāṇī ta kachī Satgurū bājhahu, hor kachī Bāṇī.
(Ādi Granth – p. 920)

Without the True Guru, speech is unripe;
words spoken without the True Guru remain immature.

These lines remind the seeker that sacred utterance must arise from realization rather than mere repetition. Words may be spoken or remembered in many ways, but only the Word grounded in truth carries the power to transform.

Within this context the emergence of written Bani takes on deeper significance. Oral teaching carried the wisdom across regions and communities, yet writing preserved that voice faithfully so its meaning could remain clear across generations.

The use of script therefore did not replace the living Shabad—it served to protect it. By giving written form to the spoken revelation of the saints, the teachings could be transmitted without distortion, allowing seekers in distant times and places to encounter the same Divine message.

The Bani itself reflects this transition from spoken realization to written preservation. References to tablets, letters, and written lessons suggest that sacred instruction was increasingly recorded so that the Divine remembrance would remain accessible to all.

Kabir expresses this devotion in simple yet powerful words:

Meṛī paṭīā likh dehu Srī Gopāl.
Nahī chhoḍau re bābā Rām Nām.
(Ādi Granth – p. 1194)

Write my lesson tablet for me, O Divine Gopal;
I shall never abandon the Name of the Lord.

In this humble request, the written tablet becomes a symbol of commitment to the Divine Name. Writing serves remembrance; remembrance awakens realization.

Through time, the sacred utterances of many realized voices were gathered and preserved within the Ādi Granth—"Ādi" signifying the primal or belonging to the beginning. In this form, the Bani stands not as the voice of a single community or identity, but as a universal message addressing all humanity.

The script in which this Bani was preserved—Gurmukhi—thus became more than a writing system. It became the vessel through which the Divine Word could be faithfully transmitted. While languages may change across generations, the Shabad carried through this script continues to guide every seeker who approaches it with sincerity.

In this way the written Bani serves as a bridge between generations. The letters preserve the sound, the sound carries remembrance, and through that remembrance the seeker encounters the eternal Shabad. Though the Divine Word transcends all letters and forms, it continues to speak through the preserved Bani, guiding every heart that listens with sincerity.

220

8. Gurmukhi Letters in Ravidass Bani

In the devotional milieu of the fifteenth century, sacred vocabulary moved from classical registers into living vernacular expression. Terms such as Sant, Satguru, Bhagat, and Sikh—rooted in earlier Sanskritic traditions (bhakta → bhagat, śiṣya → sikh, sat → sant, sadguru → satguru)—circulated widely in spoken form. In this context, sikh retained its essential meaning of a learner or disciple—one who received guidance from the Satguru.

Within gatherings of collective singing, these words acquired renewed depth, as repetition transformed inherited language into lived experience. Through such oral transmission, a stable phonetic language emerged—clear in sound, accessible in structure, and suited to communal remembrance.

When the time came to preserve this bani in written form, the script did not create this expression but served as its vessel, anchoring in letters a current of utterance that had long flowed through voice.

Larivār (ਲੜੀਵਾਰ) represents the earliest writing style of Gurmukhi, in which words appear as a continuous flow without separation, as seen in early manuscripts of the Ādi Granth. This format reflects a stage of writing closely aligned with recitation, where meaning was carried through sound and rhythm rather than visual segmentation.

Among the preserved bodies of bani, that of Ravidass provides a particularly clear example of this phonetic expression. The thirty-nine shabads attributed to him in the Ādi Granth naturally display the range of foundational Gurmukhi letters and sounds. (In some recensional traditions, a repeated shabad across rāgs brings the total to forty.) These appear organically within devotional speech rather than through constructed demonstration.

Expressions such as ਇਕੁ (ik, "one") exemplify the relationship between sound and script, where written form follows spoken pronunciation. This reflects a system grounded in living speech rather than imposed structure.

For this reason, Ravidass's bani provides a valuable illustration of how Gurmukhi letters function within devotional expression. The following table presents examples of these letters as they appear naturally within his bani, highlighting the continuity between spoken utterance and written preservation.

No.	Letter	Roman Name	Word from Bani
1.	ੳ	Ooraa	ਓਟ
2.	ਅ	Aaraa	ਅਖਰ
3.	ੲ	Iree	ਇਕੁ
4.	ਸ	Sassa	ਸਤਿਗੁਰ
5.	ਹ	Haahaa	ਹਰਿ
6.	ਕ	Kakka	ਕੰਧ
7.	ਖ	Khakhaa	ਖਰਾ
8.	ਗ	Gagga	ਗਿਆਨੀ
9.	ਘ	Ghaghaa	ਘਰ
10.	ਙ	Ngangaa	—

11.	ਚ	Chachaa	ਚਮਾਰ
12.	ਛ	Chhachaa	ਛਾਡਿ
13.	ਜ	Jajja	ਜਪੈ
14.	ਝ	Jhajhaa	ਝੂਠੈ
15.	ਞ	Nyaniaa	—
16.	ਟ	Tainkaa	ਟਰੈ
17.	ਠ	Thathaa	ਅਠਸਠਿ
18.	ਡ	Dadda	ਡਰੈ
19.	ਢ	Dhadhhaa	ਢੁਢੈ
20.	ਣ	Nhaanaa	ਗੁਣ
21.	ਤ	Tattaa	ਤੇਰਾ
22.	ਥ	Thathaa	ਥੰਭਾ
23.	ਦ	Dadda	ਦਰਸਨੁ
24.	ਧ	Dhadhhaa	ਧਨ
25.	ਨ	Naanaa	ਨਾਰਿ
26.	ਪ	Pappaa	ਪਰਸਾਦਿ
27.	ਫ	Faffaa	ਫਲ
28.	ਬ	Babbaa	ਬਰਾਬਰਿ
29.	ਭ	Bhabhaa	ਭਗਤ
30.	ਮ	Mammaa	ਮਸਹੂਰ
31.	ਯ	Yiyaa	ਬਜਾਪਾਰੁ
32.	ਰ	Raarraa	ਰਹਤ
33.	ਲ	Lallaa	ਲਾਗੀ
34.	ਵ	Vaavaa	ਵਰਤਣਿ
35.	ੜ	Rraarraa	ਪੜੀਐ

Gurmukhi Script

Following the earlier alphabetic articulation preserved in Kabir's Bāvan Akharī, later canonical compositions continued to elaborate and clarify the understanding of letters within the developing Gurmukhi tradition. These reflections demonstrate continuity rather than rupture, maintaining an ordered phonetic structure while deepening devotional meaning.

The table below presents selected letters together with their traditional explanations and phonetic values as preserved within the Ādi Granth. By comparing these stages of articulation, one can observe how the sound structure of the script remained stable while its interpretation continued to unfold within devotional reflection.

No.	Letter	Explanation	Traditional	Punjabi	Roman	Sound
1.	ੳ	ੳ	ਉੁੜੈ	ਉੁੜਾ	Ooraa	u/o
2.	ਅ	ਆਆ	ਆਇੜੈ	ਆੜਾ	Aaraa	a
3.	ੲ	ੲ	ਈਵੜੀ	ਇੜੀ	Iree	i/e
4.	ਸ	ਸਸਾ	ਸਸੈ	ਸੱਸਾ	Sassa	sa
5.	ਹ	ਹਾਹਾ	ਹਾਹੈ	ਹਾਹਾ	Haahaa	ha
6.	ਕ	ਕਕਾ	ਕਕੈ	ਕੱਕਾ	Kakka	kite
7.	ਖ	ਖਖਾ	ਖਖੈ	ਖੱਖਾ	Khakhaa	kha
8.	ਗ	ਗਗਾ	ਗਾਗੈ	ਗੱਗਾ	Gagga	go
9.	ਘ	ਘਘਾ	ਘਘੈ	ਘੱਘਾ	Ghaghaa	ga
10.	ਙ	ਙੰਙਾ	ਙੰਙੈ	ਙੰਙਾ	Ngangaa	nga
11.	ਚ	ਚਚਾ	ਚਚੈ	ਚੱਚਾ	Chachaa	chair
12.	ਛ	ਛਛਾ	ਛਛੈ	ਛੱਛਾ	Chhachaa	chha
13.	ਜ	ਜਜਾ	ਜਜੈ	ਜੱਜਾ	Jajja	jam

14.	ਝ	ਝਝਾ	ਝਝੈ	ਝੱਝਾ	Jhajhaa	jha
15.	ਞ	ਞੰਞਾ	ਞੰਞੈ	ਞੰਞਾ	Nyaniaa	Nasal nya
16.	ਟ	ਟਟਾ	ਟਟੈ	ਟੈਂਕਾ	Tainkaa	t
17.	ਠ	ਠਠਾ	ਠਠੈ	ਠੱਠਾ	Thathaa	tha
18.	ਡ	ਡਡਾ	ਡਡੈ	ਡੱਡਾ	Dadda	d
19.	ਢ	ਢਢਾ	ਢਢੈ	ਢੱਢਾ	Dhadhhaa	dha
20.	ਣ	ਣਾਣਾ	ਣਾਣੈ	ਣਾਣਾ	Nhaanaa	na
21.	ਤ	ਤਤਾ	ਤਤੈ	ਤੱਤਾ	Tattaa	ta
22.	ਥ	ਥਥਾ	ਥਥੈ	ਥੱਥਾ	Thathaa	tha
23.	ਦ	ਦਦਾ	ਦਦੈ	ਦੱਦਾ	Dadda	da
24.	ਧ	ਧਧਾ	ਧਧੈ	ਧੱਧਾ	Dhadhhaa	dha
25.	ਨ	ਨੰਨਾ	ਨੰਨੈ	ਨੱਨਾ	Naanaa	na
26.	ਪ	ਪਪਾ	ਪਪੈ	ਪੱਪਾ	Pappaa	pa
27.	ਫ	ਫਫਾ	ਫਫੈ	ਫੱਫਾ	Faffaa	pha/fa
28.	ਬ	ਬਬਾ	ਬਬੈ	ਬੱਬਾ	Babbaa	ba
29.	ਭ	ਭਭਾ	ਭਭੈ	ਭੱਭਾ	Bhabhaa	bha
30.	ਮ	ਮਮਾ	ਮੰਮੈ	ਮੱਮਾ	Mammaa	ma
31.	ਯ	ਯਜਾ	ਯਜੈ	ਯੀਆ	Yiyaa	ya
32.	ਰ	ਰਾਰਾ	ਰਾਰੈ	ਰਾਰਾ	Raarraa	ra
33.	ਲ	ਲਲਾ	ਲਲੈ	ਲੱਲਾ	Lallaa	la
34.	ਵ	ਵਾਵਾ	ਵਵੈ	ਵਾਵਾ	Vaavaa	va/wa
35.	ੜ	ੜਾੜਾ	ੜਾੜੈ	ੜਾੜਾ	Rraarraa	rra

Orthographic Development and Vowel System

Pairī bindi (nukta)—the dot placed at the foot of certain Gurmukhi letters (such as ਖ਼, ਗ਼, ਜ਼, ਫ਼, ਲ਼)—is not found in the original text of the Ādi Granth. As Gurmukhi developed over time, its orthography gradually expanded to represent additional phonetic distinctions with greater precision, and later writing conventions introduced marks such as the addak (˘) and nasal bindis (ਂ/.), which indicate consonant doubling and nasalization more explicitly.

In the canonical recension of the Ādi Granth, however, these diacritical marks are not employed in systematic form. This reflects an earlier stage of orthographic practice in which phonetic distinctions were conveyed primarily through contextual reading and established recitational tradition rather than through additional graphic signs. Contemporary editions that follow the traditional recension preserve this structural convention, maintaining continuity with early manuscript practice.

Alongside its consonantal framework, Gurmukhi employs vowel symbols (matras) to modify the inherent vowel of each consonant. These matras generate distinct vowel values and allow the formation of complete syllables. Together, consonants and vowel signs create a sound-based writing system that emphasizes phonetic clarity and rhythmic stability—features well suited to the preservation of orally transmitted bani.

The table below presents the principal vowel symbols (Matras) used in Gurmukhi and illustrates how they modify the sound of a consonant to produce different syllabic forms.

No.	Matra	Punjabi	Roman	A+Matra	Sound
1.	—	ਮੁਕਤਾ	Mukta	ਅ	a (short)
2.	ਾ	ਕੰਨਾ	Kaanaa	ਆ	aa / ā
3.	ਿ	ਸਿਹਾਰੀ	Sihaaree	ਇ	i (short)
4.	ੀ	ਬਿਹਾਰੀ	Bihaaree	ਈ	ee / ī

5.	ੌ	ਔਂਕੜ	Aukarr	ਉ	u (short)
6.	ੂ	ਦੁਲੈਂਕੜ	Dulaikarr	ਊ	oo / ū
7.	ੇ	ਲਾਂ	Laav (Lava)	ਏ	ae
8.	ੈ	ਦੁਲਾਂਵਾਂ	Dulaavaa(n)	ਐ	ai
9.	ੋ	ਹੋੜਾ	Horaa	ਓ	o
10.	ੌ	ਕਨੌੜਾ	Kanauraa	ਔ	au / aw
11.	ੱ	ਅੱਧਕ	Addak	ਅੱ	Consonant doubling
12.	ੰ	ਟਿੱਪੀ	Tippi	ੰ	an / am
13.	ਂ	ਬਿੰਦੀ	Bindi	ਂ	an / ang
14.	਼	ਨੁਕਤਾ	Nukta	ਜ਼, ਗ਼, ਖ਼	z, gh, kh
15.	ਃ	ਵਿਸਰਗ	Visarg	ਅਃ	ah
16.	।	ਇੱਕ ਡੰਡੀ	Ik Dandee	ਅੰਤ	End

Pairī̃ Akhar (Subjoined Consonants)

Pairī̃ akhar ("foot letters") are subjoined consonants used in classical Gurmukhi to represent consonant clusters and combined phonetic sounds. These forms appear beneath the primary consonant and function as structural devices that preserve precise sound values within written expression.

Among the earliest attested pairī̃ forms are pairī̃ lalla (ਲ) and pairī̃ yayya (ਯ), both visible in early manuscript traditions. The subjoined ਯ occurs in clusters such as ਕ੍ਯ and ਗ੍ਯ, while the classical ਲ appears in combinations such as ਕ੍ਲ and ਗ੍ਲ. These constructions demonstrate an orthographic system attentive to phonetic nuance while maintaining structural simplicity.

Subjoined consonants appear in older manuscript traditions and remain visible in the bani attributed to Ravidass, reflecting continuity with early Gurmukhi writing practices. Their use illustrates the script's ability to represent complex sound patterns while preserving its fundamentally phonetic character.

The table below presents common pairī̃ akhar and examples of their pronunciation within Gurmukhi combinations.

No.	Subjoined Letter	Example	Pronunciation	Roman
1.	ਰ (ਪੈਰੀਂ Rara)	ਕ੍ਰ, ਪ੍ਰ, ਤ੍ਰ	ਰ sound under letter	kra, pra, tra
2.	ਵ (ਪੈਰੀਂ Vava)	ਕ੍ਵ, ਸ੍ਵ	ਵ sound under letter	kva, sva
3.	ਜ (Yayya)	ਕਜ, ਗਾਜ	ਜ sound letter	kya, gya
4.	ਹ (ਪੈਰੀਂ Haha)	ਕ੍ਹ, ਮ੍ਹ	ਹ subtle breath sound	kha, mha
5.	ਲ (ਪੈਰੀਂ Lalla)	ਕ੍ਲ, ਗ੍ਲ	ਲ sound under letter	kla, gla

Gurmukhi Numerals

The following table presents the Gurmukhi numerals (੦–੯) alongside their Arabic and Roman equivalents. These numerals form an integral part of the traditional writing system and demonstrate that Gurmukhi functioned not only as a script for sacred utterance but also as a practical system for everyday record and notation.

Placed alongside modern numerical conventions, the traditional forms reveal the continuity between historical Punjabi literacy and contemporary usage. Like the letters, vowel signs, and subjoined consonants, the numeral system reflects the structural completeness of Gurmukhi as a fully developed writing tradition.

No.	Gurmukhi	Arabic	Roman
1.	੦	0	—
2.	੧	1	I
3.	੨	2	II

4.	੩	3	III
5.	੪	4	IV
6.	੫	5	V
7.	੬	6	VI
8.	੭	7	VII
9.	੮	8	VIII
10.	੯	9	IX

Taken together—the consonants, vowel signs (matras), subjoined forms (pairī akhar), and numerals—Gurmukhi appears as a complete and coherent writing system shaped around sound. Its structure reflects organic refinement within a devotional environment where speech preceded inscription and recitation guided writing. In this sense, Gurmukhi—"from the mouth of the Guru"—may be understood as voice preserved in visible form: utterance carried into script without losing its cadence.

Thus the discussion closes not merely with letters and numbers, but with the enduring principle they serve—the safeguarding of sacred speech across generations. What remains is not simply a script, but the living remembrance of the voice that gave it meaning—a voice that continues to call humanity toward truth, equality, and fearless spiritual vision.

— ✧ —

ਨਰਪਤਿ ਏਕੁ ਸਿੰਘਾਸਨਿ ਸੋਇਆ ਸੁਪਨੇ ਭਇਆ ਭਿਖਾਰੀ ॥
ਅਛਤ ਰਾਜ ਬਿਛੁਰਤ ਦੁਖੁ ਪਾਇਆ ਸੋ ਗਤਿ ਭਈ ਹਮਾਰੀ ॥

What we seek is not lost—only forgotten.
Like the dreamer, we wander in illusion,
while the kingdom remains within.

Nothing is missing

Sources Consulted

Primary Scriptures and Devotional Texts

- Ādi Granth — Early manuscript and recension tradition (Consulted through multiple manuscript lineages and bir traditions) Present form: Sri Guru Granth Sahib Ji (SGGS)
- Bhagavad Gītā — Traditional scripture
- Valmiki Rāmāyaṇa — Epic tradition attributed to Maharishi Valmiki
- The Buddha and His Dhamma — B. R. Ambedkar
- The Diary of Bhagwan — Spiritual reflections attributed to Sri Bhagwan
- Bījak — Kabir Panth textual tradition
- Ravidass Deep Granth — By Saint Hira Dass
- Abhaṅgās of Namdev — Devotional poetry attributed to Namdev
- Amrit Bani — Satguru Ravidass Ji (Traditional compilation)
- Sant Ravidass kī Vāṇī kā Saṅgīt Mādhurya — By Madhubala Saxena
- Param Pāras: Guru Ravidass — As described in the literature by Kashinath Upadhyay
- Mira Bai Ki Padāvalī — Edited by Parashuram Chaturvedi
- Vāraṅ Bhāī Gurdāss — By Bhai Gurdass (traditional attribution)
- Santhya: Sri Guru Granth Sahib Ji — By Bhai Vir Singh (Consulted across multiple volumes and editions)
- Kabīr Granthāvalī — Published by Nagari Pracharini Sabha

Bhakti Hagiographical Literature

- Bhaktamāl — Traditional Bhakti hagiographical text attributed to Nabha Das; consulted in this work through multiple recensions, editions, and commentarial traditions.

- Bhaktamāl Ṭīkā — Traditional commentary on Bhaktamāl by Priyadas.
- The Parcaī-s of Anantadās — As edited, translated, and studied by Winand M. Callewaert.

Scholarly and Historical Studies

- The Life and Works of Raidas — By Winand M. Callewaert and Peter G. Friedlander
- Dictionary of Bhakti — By Winand M. Callewaert (with the assistance of Swapna Sharma)
- Negotiating Religion; Unit XI: Religious Ideas and Movements — By Rameshwar Prasad Bahuguna
- Sangarshi Jodhe — Dr. S. L. Virdi
- Adi Dharm Movement and Babu Mangu Ram Mugowalia — Dr. Ronki Ram

Origins and Evolution of Gurmukhi Script

- Gurmukhī Lipī dā Janam te Vikās — By S. G. B. Singh
- Gurmukhī Lipī dā Itihās — By Piyara Singh Padam
- Pañjābī Bhāshā dā Vikās — By Duni Chand

www.ingramcontent.com/pod-product-compliance
Lightning Source LLC
Chambersburg PA
CBHW030054110726
47973CB00002B/21